·E·X·P·L·O·R·E·
M·U·S·K·O·K·A

· E·X·P·L·O·R·E ·
M·U·S·K·O·K·A

Susan Pryke

The BOSTON
MILLS PRESS

CANADIAN CATALOGUING IN PUBLICATION DATA
Pryke, Susan, 1952-
Explore Muskoka

ISBN 0-919783-90-2

1. Muskoka (Ont.: District municipality) - Description and travel - Tours.
2. History - Ontario - Muskoka. 3. Automobiles - Ontario -
Muskoka (District municipality) Touring.   1. Title.

FC3095.M9P79 1987   917.13'16044   C87-094378-2
FlO59.M9P79 1987

03 02 01 00 99   2 3 4 5 6

Reprinted in 1999 by
BOSTON MILLS PRESS
132 Main Street
Erin, Ontario N0B 1T0
Tel 519-833-2407
Fax 519-833-2195
e-mail books@boston-mills.on.ca
www.boston-mills.on.ca

An affiliate of
STODDART PUBLISHING CO. LIMITED
34 Lesmill Road
Toronto, Ontario, Canada
M3B 2T6
Tel 416-445-3333
Fax 416-445-5967
e-mail gdsinc@genpub.com

Distributed in Canada by
General Distribution Services Limited
325 Humber College Boulevard
Toronto, Canada M9W 7C3
Orders 1-800-387-0141 Ontario & Quebec
Orders 1-800-387-0172
NW Ontario & Other Provinces
e-mail customer.service@ccmailgw.genpub.com

EDI Canadian Telebook S1150391
Distributed in the United States by
General Distribution Services Inc.
85 River Rock Drive, Suite 202
Buffalo, New York 14207-2170
Toll-free 1-800-805-1083
Toll-free fax 1-800-481-6207
e-mail gdsinc@genpub.com

Boston Mills Press gratefully acknowledges the Canada Council for the Arts,
the Government of Canada through the Book Publishing Industry Development Program (BPIDP),
and the Ontario Arts Council for their support of our publishing program.

Edited by Noel Hudson
Design by Gill Stead
Map illustrations by Mary Firth
Commissioned photography by G.W. Campbell

Printed in Canada

Contents

ACKNOWLEDGMENTS

So many people helped make this book possible; some by sharing photographs and information, others by lending their support. In this latter category, I wish to express my appreciation to the Ontario Arts Council for financial assistance, and to my publisher, John Denison, who liked the idea from the start. Also, to my husband, David Pryke, for his honest, perceptive comments on the manuscript, and his unfailing belief and support. In addition, I would like to acknowledge the assistance of the following people:

Charles Amey
Eleanor Andrew
Rheta Asbury
R.J. Boyer
Linda Brett
Betty Campbell
Heather Coupland
Peggy Crowder
Paul Davidson
Tony Davidson
Jean Dickson
John Dixon
Cyril and Marion Fry
Robert Geddes
Mary Hardy
Lindsay Hill
Dr. Norris (Joe) Hunt
Maureen Hunt

Arthur Hutcheson
Jack Hutton
Lorne Jewitt
George Johnson
Laura Kennedy
Jack Laycock
Elizabeth Langford
Gary Long
Niall MacKay
Doug McCulley
Betty Maynard
Violet McCann
Joyce McClellan
Hugh MacLennan
Beryl Munro
Doreen Nowak
Barb Paterson
Dudley Penney

Oscar Purdy
Bertha Robertson
Fred Schulz
Ed Skinner
Bill Snider
Ernest Stanton
Isabel Swainson
Paul Tapley
Ian Turnbull
Viola Vanclieaf
Dave Villard
Paul White
Emily Wood
Jim Wood
Peter Wood
Jamie Woodruff
Carole Young

Preface

About the Book ...

It's not so much what I found but what I *didn't* find that got me interested in this project. You can blame the Portage Train — that miniature locomotive that once ran on the world's shortest rail line between Peninsula Lake and Lake of Bays. It intrigued me to hear that it ran backward as well as forward, and that it travelled at such a snail's pace people could jump off and pick berries. But when I went looking for it, for where it used to be, I could find no trace. There were no plaques or markers to indicate the significance of the site.

To satisfy my curiosity, I found a man who could point out exactly where everything had been. Jack Laycock stood me on spots where the ties were still visible and where the remains of an old steamer were buried under my feet. I thought to myself: "That's information everyone should know." Not only about the Portage Railway, but about other historic sites that are mouldering away by the roadsides. Beauty spots and recreational settings, too. Voilà!

The Book . . .

Explore Muskoka was written with three separate audiences in mind. First, the people who live in Muskoka, or spend their summers here, to show them what interesting excursions exist in their own backyard. It's also for the tourists who come to Muskoka on vacation or day trips, to guide them on sightseeing expeditions. There's an invisible audience, as well; those people who may pick up the book in a place far away from Muskoka. For those people, the book is a lure, an invitation to come to this most beautiful and historic lakeland.

What The Book Does ...

Explore Muskoka pinpoints locations that I've found interesting, intriguing or beautiful. The maps are a key feature. Without them you may learn about Muskoka; with them you can experience the district. There's a big difference.

The book should also deal the final blow to the misconception that there's not enough to see and do in Muskoka. Now when your Aunt Martha arrives, you can hop in the car and tour the lakes, stopping every now and then at places you hadn't realized existed. There's so much to see and do, in fact, that I've had to split several tours into manageable blocks.

At the beginning of each tour there's an indication of distance. There's also a summary of the major attractions and scenic locations you'll pass on the way, plus a list of antique shops and arts and crafts studios. I've included these because many sightseers are also browsers and shoppers, and because the places mentioned have character and charm. The shops are ones I'm personally familiar with and have enjoyed. There are others I've yet to discover. The proliferation of unique arts and crafts shops reflects the character of the people and the district. People who paint, carve and weave find Muskoka an inspirational place to live. That, in itself, says a great deal about the landscape and the lifestyle you find here.

What The Book Does Not Do ...

Explore Muskoka has a definite historical slant because I enjoy looking at today's world through "yesterday" glasses. But it is not a history book in the true sense of the word, nor is it a travel guide that lists every bait-and-tackle place, every restaurant, every dry cleaners from the Severn River to Arrowhead Park. It is a combination of the two, with a little more emphasis on history than modern activities.

As most of Muskoka's history has been expertly recorded, I have not tried to redo the work. I've concentrated, instead, on snippets of history as they relate to the view from your car window and added my own impressions of each location.

— THE TOWNS —

The most difficult task in writing this book came in trimming down the information I'd collected about the towns in Muskoka. There's so much to write about Huntsville, Bracebridge and Gravenhurst that each could have a tour book of its own. I chose, instead, to select a route through each town, and restrict my comments to those sights and attractions along the way. If you are interested in exploring the towns further, stop by the information centres listed below.

Gravenhurst Chamber of Commerce
295-1 Muskoka Road South
Gravenhurst, P1P 1J1
705-687-4432

Bracebridge Chamber of Commerce
1-1 Manitoba Street
Bracebridge, P1L 1S4
705-645-8121

Huntsville Lake of Bays Chamber of Commerce
8 West Street North
Huntsville, P1H 2B6
705-789-4771

—THE RESORTS —

Muskoka is Ontario's most popular destination area so there many resorts and tourist establishments. In this book, I've mentioned those that stand out because of their style, reputation or historical significance.

Muskoka Tourism has information on every resort, hotel, motel and campground in Muskoka. The year-round office is located in Severn Bridge.

Muskoka Tourism
RR 2
Kilworthy
P0E 1G0
1-800-267-9700

— TOUR MAPS —

The tour maps show, at a glance, where each point of interest is along the route. Kilometre readings are indicated between each point of interest or intersection. Separate maps are included for communities and towns.

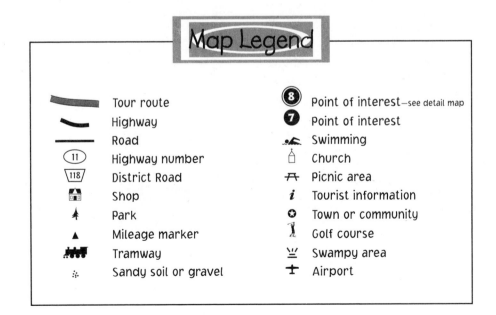

	Map Legend		
	Tour route	⑧	Point of interest—see detail map
	Highway	❼	Point of interest
	Road		Swimming
⑪	Highway number		Church
118	District Road		Picnic area
	Shop	*i*	Tourist information
	Park		Town or community
▲	Mileage marker		Golf course
	Tramway		Swampy area
	Sandy soil or gravel		Airport

Family grouping at Windermere. You can just see Windermere House in the background. This is an early picture of the resort, when it had just one tower. MUSKOKA LAKES MUSEUM

INTRODUCTION

The Face of Muskoka

"Many settlers after passing through the rocky country between Washago and
Bracebridge and still finding rocks staring them in the face, get discouraged or
homesick; and, without going into the country to see what it is like, pick up
their traps and leave by the first steamer ... I must say that the rocks have
rather a chilling effect at first sight on those who are not used to them."

Albert Sydney-Smith
Letter to the Editor
Stratford *Beacon*, 11 July 1871

Y ou notice the difference as soon as you cross the Severn River. After the
rolling farmland and neat woodlots of Southern Ontario, the hard rocks
of Muskoka loom out of the landscape like a cold shrug of the earth's
primordial shoulders. You've entered Canadian Shield Country.

Imagine how the pioneers felt when they encountered this muscular
terrain — so different from the pliant soils of their homelands. Time and again
reports mention settlers "closing their eyes" to the rocks and trusting the
promise of the majestic forests.

Back then, people believed that good stands of timber meant good soil for
farming. In Southern Ontario that theory proved true. The settlers cleared the
land and cultivated productive fields. Over the years clearing and cultivation
exposed the long, smooth slopes you see when you travel north from Toronto.
Underneath it all is an abundance of flat limestone slabs that weather easily
and help build good soils.

Muskoka was different. It had impressive stands of timber, but the soils
were shallow layers built on less permeable rock. When the settlers felled the
trees to "improve" the land, they took away the very things that had nourished
and protected it for thousands of years. The ensuing erosion exposed Muskoka
as a rocky fastness — a landscape unlike anything you'll find south of the
Severn River.

In spite of (and perhaps because of) the heartache the rocks engendered,
they've become the persona of Muskoka. Ripped through by dynamite, they
tower snaggle-toothed over the roadways, taking your breath away as you whiz
by them. Just as maritimers miss the sea when they've left it, so Muskokans
miss the rocks when they're away from home. Other landscapes seem tame by
comparison. There's a comfort to the rocks, as well: a faithful solidity.

The prevalence of the rock throughout Muskoka makes it appear commonplace, but its pedigree is impressive. The Canadian Shield is the exposed rock core of the North American continent. Eons ago the original rock melted and recrystallized deep in the earth's crust. Geologists have dated samples of Muskoka rock back 1.5 billion years, and it is possible that some of the rocks are over two billion years old. What brings that time frame into focus is the knowledge that these features were once buried by 30 kilometres of rock — rock which has, with infinite patience, eroded away.

While the rocks are the substance of Muskoka, the lakes are its spirit. Seen from the air, the waterways weave Muskoka together in a crystal blue web. There are over 1,600 lakes in all, each one sparkling and winking in the sunshine, tempting visitors to dive in and enjoy them. The lakes have been the focus of the tourism industry since steamboat days. Over the years their significance has been incorporated in slogans: first "Land of Clear Skies and Many Waters," then "Land of the Pleasure Lakes." Today it's "Muskoka — the Greatest Lakes." The emphasis has always been on water.

The luxuriance of Muskoka's lakes is the legacy of four separate glaciations. Walls of ice several kilometres thick crunched across the bedrock and gouged out dips and valleys. After the ice sheets retreated, the meltwaters poured off the Algonquin Highlands, spilling from one basin to another, working their way to Georgian Bay.

Crisscrossing the district as they did, the waterways became the transportation arteries for the new settlements that sprang up after the Free Grants and Homestead Act of 1868. The act was introduced to encourage settlement in the north. Years before, there had been thoughts of making Muskoka a vast Indian reservation. The tide of immigration into Southern Ontario, coupled with the awareness of Muskoka's rich timber reserves, forced officials to reconsider.

The Free Grants and Homestead Act gave 200 acres of land to families who settled in Muskoka, with extra land granted to compensate for rocky sections. In return the settler had to clear 15 acres of land, build a house, and live on the site continuously for five years. At that time, if he'd complied with the government's wishes, he could apply for his land patent. These stipulations were made to discourage speculation. The government retained possession of the riches of the land: the pine trees, the quarry stones and mineral wealth.

The interests of the settlers took a back seat to the interests of the lumbermen in the early days. The government could, and did, grant timber licences on a settler's land. There was nothing a settler could do about it, nor about the logging roads that churned across his property. The settler, himself, had to pay the same government dues that the loggers did if he cut down more

In the heyday of lumbering, Muskoka Bay was so full of logs "you could walk across it."
The Rathbun sawmill, shown here, was one of many mills built in Gravenhurst.
GRAVENHURST ARCHIVES

than his 30-acre allowance of timber. On the other hand, the settlers could not have survived without the lumber industry. Heartsick from the backbreaking labour they'd put into unproductive, rocky farmland, the settlers joined logging camps over the winter months to make ends meet. For their own part, the lumbermen were so intent on cutting down the forests that they eventually logged themselves out of business.

Muskoka, true to form, survived the decline of both farming and lumbering. Like the cat with nine lives, she landed firmly on her feet. Tourists had discovered the invigorating atmosphere of the lakeland. They could canoe, fish, swim and bask in the sunshine. Cares and worries dissolved in crystal waters. The clear, woodsy air had the power to restore the sick and rejuvenate the weary. What's more, this palliative of body and soul was as close to the big city as a day's trip on the trains and steamboats.

Today it's this same combination of rustic beauty, convenience and closeness to the major centres that makes Muskoka one of the most popular tourist destinations in Ontario. The intensity of spirit remains, but it's the pursuit of leisure activities, not lumbering, which now drives people to the hinterlands of Muskoka — and this time they're taking better care to preserve their greatest natural resources, the landscape and the lakes.

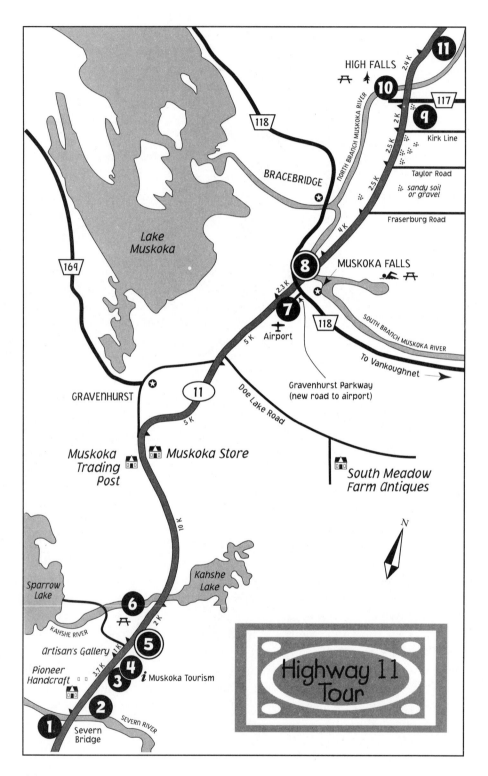

HIGH FALLS

11

10

117

9

Kirk Line

2.4 K

2 K

2.5 K

NORTH BRANCH MUSKOKA RIVER

118

BRACEBRIDGE

2.5 K

Taylor Road

sandy soil
or gravel

4 K

Fraserburg Road

Lake
Muskoka

169

8 MUSKOKA FALLS

2.3 K

7

Airport

118

SOUTH BRANCH MUSKOKA RIVER

To Vankoughnet

5 K

Gravenhurst Parkway
(new road to airport)

GRAVENHURST

11

Doe Lake Road

5 K

Muskoka
Trading
Post

Muskoka Store

South Meadow
Farm Antiques

N

10 K

Kahshe
Lake

Sparrow
Lake

6

Kahshe
Lake

KAHSHE RIVER

2 K

Artisan's Gallery

1.1 K

5

Pioneer
Handcraft

3.7 K

4

3

_i_ Muskoka Tourism

2

1

Severn
Bridge

SEVERN RIVER

Highway 11
Tour

CHAPTER 1

Highway 11 Tour

Severn Bridge, Muskoka Falls, High Falls
Distance: 43 kilometres (26 miles)

S tarting at the Severn River, this tour retraces the steps of the pioneers who journeyed north along the Muskoka Colonization Road. Highway 11, for the most part, follows the original roadway from Severn Bridge to Muskoka Falls.

It's a stretch of roadway that everyone travels, but few investigate because of the cement barrier and its "go with the flow" design. Although Highway 11 is a busy thoroughfare, it has some interesting sights to watch for, including Ontario's own Rock of Gibraltar and the sandy shoreline of an ancient lake. The route also claims two of the most dramatic waterfalls in Muskoka: South Falls and High Falls.

— Sights —

Muskoka Colonization Road
   Historic Marker
Peterson Road Historic Marker
South Falls
Muskoka Airport
High Falls
Bracebridge Resource
   Management Trails

— Antiques —

South Meadow Farm Antiques
Follow signs from intersection of
Highway 11 and Doe Lake Road
705-687-2660

— Arts and Crafts —

Pioneer Handcraft
Highway 11 S
705-689-2604

Artisan's Gallery
Highway 11 S
705-689-6121

The Muskoka Store
Highway 11 N
705-687-7751

Muskoka Trading Post
Highway 11 S
705-687-4809

Getting from here to there wasn't as easy in the early days.
ONTARIO ARCHIVES 15808-88

SEVERN BRIDGE HIGHLIGHTS

While Gravenhurst claims to be Muskoka's first town, Severn Bridge is really where it all began. Prior to the 1840s there seemed no reason to push colonization any farther than the Severn River. The pathfinders who crisscrossed Muskoka did so for military and commercial reasons. They were searching for an alternative water route to the Great Lakes system, while keeping an eye open for evidence of mineral wealth and land assets.

A swelling stream of immigration helped push back the frontiers. In the 1850s that stream spilled into Muskoka. Surveyors established the route of the Colonization Road from Severn Bridge to Muskoka Falls and work began in 1858.

As an entry point to the district, Severn Bridge became a pivotal community, with several hotels, stores, a church, school and community hall. Locating agent R.J. Oliver came to Severn Bridge in 1859 and gave the first settlers the tickets to their land claims. Many had arrived a year or more before and had been squatting on land along the proposed Colonization Road. Land along the roadway, although accessible, was not really suitable for farming.

Those settlers who ventured farther into the bush found better land in the western sections of Morrison Township near Sparrow Lake. Here communities of Germans and Scots wrestled good farms out of the wilderness around them.

As with most Muskoka communities, lumbering played an important role in growth and development. Smith and Ball built the first sawmill in 1869 on the southwest side of the river. The mill passed through several hands until it was swallowed by lumbering giant Mickle-Dyment, who set up a large branch plant on the Severn River. During those days, Mickle-Dyment boom logs stretched up and down the Severn River, leaving only a narrow passage for navigation.

1   THE BRIDGE OVER THE SEVERN RIVER

The importance of the bridge to the surrounding area is reflected in the naming of the village. Contractors built the bridge in 1857. At that time it linked a rough logging track, which led to Washago Mills, with the starting point of the Colonization Road.

This bridge deteriorated in short order. After a series of repairs and replacements, it was rebuilt in steel in the mid 1890s — a costly venture considering it was the first steel bridge of its size ever constructed by the County of Simcoe. Over the years other structures have been built, moving the bridge location a little to the east of its original position. The old bridge abutments are still visible downstream.

2   SEVERN RIVER INN

In 1858 James H. Jackson built a log shanty by the Severn River, near the site of the present Severn River Inn. Jackson's little cabin evolved into a general store and post office. It was, in fact, the first post office in Muskoka when Jackson received his appointment as postmaster on December 11, 1860. A fire destroyed the original building in 1906, along with most of the others on the north side of the river. The following year, James Jackson II built a brick store and boarding house on the same site as his father's old store. The Jackson family continued operating the business until James II died in 1942.

In 1981 J. Ross Raymond purchased the building and began restoring it. Under the Ontario Heritage Act, the Severn River Inn has been designated a building of architectural and historical importance. With its old-fashioned glass storefront and pillared verandah, the building is a typical and well-preserved example of a pioneer general store and inn. The main dining room is situated in the parlour of the old inn, which is furnished with antiques and reproductions that typify the early 1900s. The chance to dine in the old house, so steeped in history, makes for a memorable dining experience.

3   MUSKOKA TOURISM INFORMATION CENTRE

If you're looking for things to see and places to stay in Muskoka, this is the place to start. The Tourism Centre has all the information you are likely to need under one roof. Book your hotel room, buy tickets for events, pick up maps and information brochures. For those families who'd really like to stretch their legs after the trip from the city, there's a five-kilometre hiking trail through the Kahshe Barrens. For information, call 1-800-267-9700 or visit their web site at http://www.muskoka-tourism.on.ca.

4   BETHEL CEMETERY

Adjacent to the Tourism Centre is Muskoka's first cemetery and a monument commemorating the early pioneers of Morrison Township. The first burial in Bethel Cemetery was that of James Hanna. During a wild ride along the plank road, Hanna's horse caught its hoof and threw him. Prior to this unfortunate death, people had been claiming that Muskoka was such a healthy place to live, they'd have to kill a man to start a cemetery.

5   CUTHBERT'S STONE FORTRESS AT GIBRALTAR

Just past the Sparrow Lake Route D overpass, at the entrance to a private drive, is the precipice known as Gibraltar. The rock is lost in underbrush now, but in the 1870s it supported a stone fort erected by the Scotsman James Cuthbert. Cuthbert built the fort of boulders to imitate those he'd seen in his homeland. He stuck logs through the portholes and blackened their ends to resemble cannons.

Cuthbert earned his living as a shoemaker. Around his home he had beautiful flower gardens and an arched entranceway over which hung the sign "Gibraltar" — which accounts for the naming of the rock.

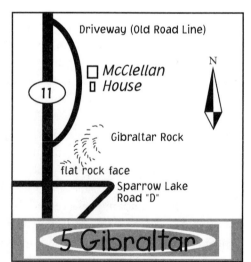

Finding a lifelike fort in the middle of nowhere caused a flurry of excitement among travellers, including the Honourable John Carling, Minister of Public Works. Carling made frequent trips to Muskoka in connection with the opening of the waterways at Port Carling and Port Sandfield. On

James Cuthbert's home at Gibraltar with stone fort and cannons in the background.
PHOTO COURTESY OF JOYCE MCCLELLAN

one of these trips Carling got down from his stage and had a close look at the fortifications. He so admired the little fort that he sent Cuthbert a real cannon.

From then on, whenever visiting dignitaries made their way into Muskoka, they'd receive a surprise salute from Cuthbert's cannon — the last thing they'd expect, I'm sure, along a rickety plank road.

6   KAHSHE RIVER AND MUSKOKA COLONIZATION ROAD
    (Historic Marker)

The park area is cut off from northbound traffic by a cement highway barrier, but it can be reached by driving to the next overpass and backtracking along the southbound lane. The new highway has bitten into the falls and eaten up some of its beauty. Still, it's a pleasant place to stop, and it provides an opportunity to meander along the shores of the Kahshe River (a shortened version of its Indian name, Kah-she-she-bog-a-mog, which means "Lake of Many islands"). The lake is situated to the east of the highway.

An historic marker commemorates the construction, in 1858, of the Muskoka Colonization Road, the most successful and enduring of the "settlement" thoroughfares of its era. As R.J. Boyer points out in his book *Early Exploration and Surveying of Muskoka District*, the route chosen for the Muskoka Road determined the location of villages and set the course for the movement of goods and supplies into the district — and still does.

Vernon Wadsworth described the road from Washago to Gravenhurst in those early days as being little better than a blazed trail, with rocks, stumps and fallen trees cluttering the way. In low, swampy areas workmen placed logs one beside the other. These corduroy roads, so called because of their resemblance to the ridges on corduroy fabric, made travelling such a back-wrenching experience that many preferred to walk. The situation improved somewhat with plank roads — which were said to have increased the lives of horses twofold.

To build a plank road the workmen first laid down log stringers and spiked the planks tightly together on top of them (much as you'd imagine a wooden bridge would be built). Then they spread a layer of sand over the planks. The problem with these roads was that the planks rotted quickly, and if they weren't replaced they could make travelling as dangerous and uncomfortable as before.

The road received its first paved surface in 1930 following an earlier move by the provincial government to take over municipal roads. The Muskoka Road became the Ferguson Highway in honour of Ontario's Conservative premier, Howard Ferguson. When the Liberals were elected in 1934 they removed all traces of Conservative favour and introduced the practice of numbering highways.

7   MUSKOKA AIRPORT

Built during the Depression years to generate employment, the Muskoka Airport was originally designed as an emergency landing strip for unscheduled stops between major airports. Work on the grass runways began in 1933.

During World War Two, the Norwegian Air Force leased the airport to train fighter pilots. The Norwegians set up camp at the far end of the field in 1942 and built hangars, dormitories, recreational facilities, a drill hall and hospital. For the duration of the war the airport was known as Little Norway. After the war the buildings became the site of a minimum-security prison called Beaver Creek Correctional Camp. A plaque commemorating the Norwegian Air Force can be found near the terminal building.

The Department of National Defence built a 6,000-foot paved runway, beginning in 1951, to support the RCAF Sabre jet fighter training base in North Bay.

Today, the airport provides ready access to Muskoka for those businessmen and vacationers who would rather fly than drive. On October 31, 1996, the District of Muskoka purchased the airport from Transport Canada for $1, to prevent it from being closed. Since that time, the airport's reputation has grown through marketing initiatives such as the annual Muskoka Air Show, which features spectacular flying demonstrations by both vintage and modern airplanes.

(To access the airport, leave the highway at Muskoka Road 118, then turn right at Gravenhurst Parkway.)

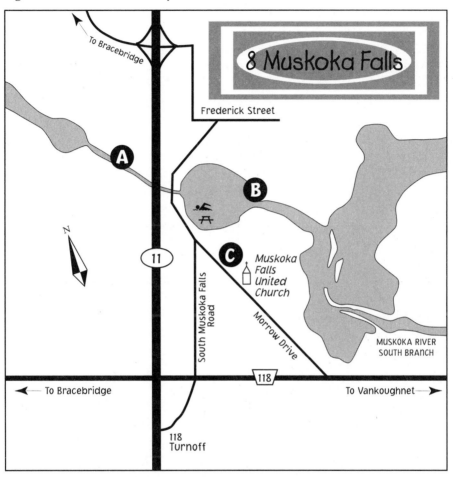

8   MUSKOKA FALLS

In pioneer days Muskoka Falls and Bracebridge each had the opportunity to become the destination town in mid-Muskoka. The community of Muskoka Falls is located on the south branch of the Muskoka River, while Bracebridge is on the north branch. In early references, surveyors distinguished the two with the names South Falls (Muskoka Falls) and North Falls (Bracebridge).

Each community was situated on the survey line for the Muskoka Colonization Road. From a settler's point of view, Muskoka Falls had the most auspicious beginnings as it marked the intersection of the colonization roads from both the south (Muskoka Colonization Road) and the east (the Peterson Road). The Peterson Road cut east through the province, making connections with the Ottawa River. Muskoka Falls pioneer Richard Hanna contracted to build the road in 1858.

In 1862 Richard Hanna opened the Muskoka Falls Post Office. The following year the settlers asked that a town site be created. W.H. Deane surveyed the site and filed the plan under the name Muskokaville, thus providing the fuel for a modern-day debate concerning whether the community should be called Muskoka Falls or Muskokaville. Local resident and historian Heather Coupland supports the Muskoka Falls case, and backs up her position with drawers full of historic documents that show the name Muskoka Falls used in every instance.

By the 1870s many settlers along the Peterson Road had abandoned their poor farms, and portions of the roadway became clogged with weeds and saplings. Muskoka settlers kept the western section of the road open to Vankoughnet. The deterioration of the Peterson Road and the advent of steam navigation on Lake Muskoka in 1866 shifted the focus to Bracebridge.

8A SOUTH FALLS

If your only glimpse of South Falls has been a sideways glance to the west as you've whizzed by on Highway 11, you're in for a surprise when you see the waterfall up close in the spring. Follow the canoe portage as it descends to the pit of the gorge. The falls cut through a narrow canyon and spill into a pretty bay. Thick-trunked pine trees cling to the steep slopes. If it weren't for the hum of the South Falls generating station at the bottom, or the intrusion of the sluice pipes feeding it, you could imagine that this is how Muskoka first appeared to the early settlers.

A postcard view of the basin below South Falls, showing the log slide.
PHOTO COURTESY OF THE MUSKOKA LAKES MUSEUM

Legendary explorer David Thompson made the first mention of this waterfall in his 1837 journals. He'd been sent by the Canadian government to explore a possible route for a canal between Georgian Bay and the Ottawa River. But he was not the first to explore the length of this river, with its interminable waterfalls and rapids. Lieutenant Henry Briscoe, of the Royal Engineers, ascended the South Muskoka way back in 1826. His was the first recorded exploration of Muskoka.

The falls, though picturesque, caused headaches for lumbermen when logs jammed in crevices, causing delays and damage. In the late 1870s the government built a log slide bypassing South Falls. Its

A torrent of water thunders through the chute at South Falls. SUSAN PRYKE PHOTO

construction drew crowds of onlookers. When it came time to try out the new contraption, a workman jumped aboard the first log and rode it down the slide, but his foolhardy stunt killed him.

The Town of Gravenhurst built the South Falls generating station at the base of the falls in 1907. Ontario Hydro took it over at a later date and expanded the facilities.

8B HANNA CHUTE

The Hanna Chute Power House is the cement structure you see when you look across the water from the Muskoka Falls Beach. The land adjoining it belonged to pioneer settler and roadbuilder Richard Hanna. It was built in 1926.

8C UNITED CHURCH AND PETERSON COLONIZATION ROAD
(Historic Marker)

If you backtrack a little into the village of Muskoka Falls, you'll find a plaque which details the history of the Peterson Colonization Road. The plaque is in front of the Muskoka Falls United Church, one of the oldest churches in Muskoka still in continuous use. The church building dates back to 1869, although it was not officially dedicated until 1871. At that time it served both the Methodists and Presbyterians. The two denominations became a single congregation when the union movement created the United Church. An interesting feature of the church is its reversible pews, which can be turned to face either direction.

The church was built at the junction of two of the early colonization roads, Muskoka Road (which ran south to north) and the Peterson Road (running east to west). The Peterson Road, named after surveyor Joseph Peterson, traversed 114 miles between Muskoka Falls and the Opeongo Road. The road failed to attract many settlers and fell into disuse, except for the stretch from Muskoka Falls to Vankoughnet. In 1972, a new road (now named Muskoka Road 118 East) was built. It roughly follows the old Peterson Road.

To continue the tour, join Highway 11 via Seventh and Frederick streets and travel north.

9   EVIDENCE OF GLACIAL LAKE ALGONQUIN

As you travel north to the Muskoka Road 117 turnoff, watch for sandy banks along the east side of the highway. The sand deposits are ancient deltas, which were created when meltwater channels entered glacial Lake Algonquin.

During the Pleistocene Epoch at least four separate glaciers crunched across Muskoka. The last ice sheet began melting about 12,000 years ago. The ice front retreated at a rate of about 130 to 140 metres per year. As the ice melted, a lake formed. The boundaries of Lake Algonquin were similar to, but extended beyond, the present boundaries of Lake Huron. The Georgian Bay shoreline pushed inland, covering the present-day Muskoka lakes.

The edge of Lake Algonquin aligns roughly parallel to and just east of Highway 11. You'll see remnants of sandy shoreline as you drive along. The coast of Lake Algonquin traced an irregular pattern around peninsulas and islands. The land along this stretch of highway was part of a narrow bay fed by a meltwater channel. The meltwater left deposits of sand and gravel at its mouth before emptying into the main body of Lake Algonquin.

In deeper areas of the lake, represented by low areas along the Highway 11 corridor, sediments of clay, silt and sand built up. In the summer a coarse, light silt settled down to the bottom of the glacial lake; in the winter the sediment was a dark, thin clay. This created annual bands of light and dark sediment called varves. Some of the varves are well exposed along Highway 11 and you can count them as you would rings on a tree trunk. In this fashion, geologists have shown that glacial Lake Algonquin covered much of Muskoka for about 900 years.

To visit High Falls, exit at the Muskoka Road 117 ramp and cross to the west side of the highway.

10 HIGH FALLS

Many cups of tea have been brewed at High Falls park. The continued popularity of the spot is evidenced in the numerous picnic spots provided for summer travellers.

Writer Gary Long says High Falls is unique: "It is the only falls in Muskoka that can honestly be called a falls." Other "falls" (correctly called "chutes") cascade through rocky chasms in a series of steps.

A short distance from High Falls, there's a cairn erected in the memory of Aubrey White, a Muskoka pioneer who created Ontario's fire ranger system in 1885.

Follow the path below the cairn and you'll find a Hobbit's paradise. The sun's rays scarcely penetrate the thick evergreens bows. The landscape is twisted into strange shapes by a mass of tree roots that seem to knit the rocks together. A mini-falls trickles through the bush at this point. If you're brave enough you can ford the stream and work your way down the slope to the sandy beach, where you'll often find huge logs washed up along the shore.

High Falls, North Branch Muskoka River.

High Falls is the truest waterfall in Muskoka. The others are more correctly called chutes.
POSTCARD COURTESY OF IAN TURNBULL

11 BRACEBRIDGE RESOURCE MANAGEMENT CENTRE

I almost hate to tell you about the Bracebridge Resource Management Centre because it will let the secret out. There wasn't a soul in the 607 hectares while I was there in August; just me, the squirrels and the cicadas buzzing in the trees.

The Bracebridge Recreational Trails Committee maintains the eight-kilometre trail system, which meanders along the Muskoka River in places.

The area was settled in 1868-1872 by 12 families who farmed and logged the property. In 1954 the Patterson brothers of Bracebridge purchased the land as a game preserve. The Crown acquired the property in 1966 as a site to demonstrate resource management techniques. Signs along the route highlight points of interest. My favourite is a huge boulder called a glacial erratic, which was carried to this spot during the ice age.

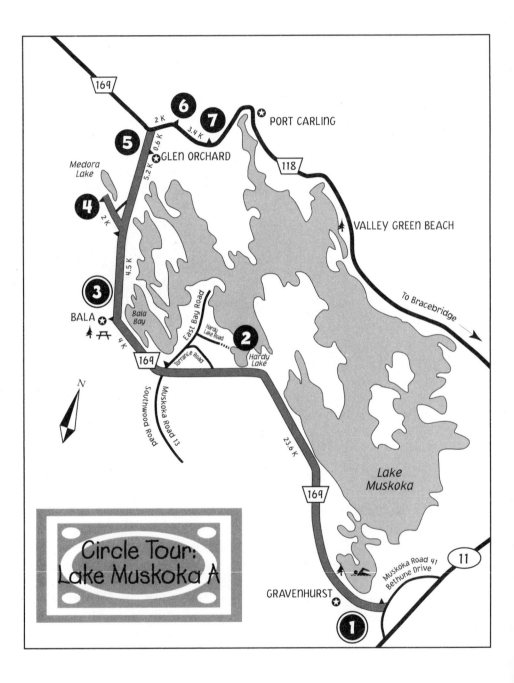

169

6
7
PORT CARLING
2 K
5
0.6 K
3.4 K
Medora
Lake
GLEN ORCHARD
5.2 K
118
4
2 K
VALLEY GREEN BEACH
4.5 K
To Bracebridge
3
BALA
East Bay Road
Bala
Bay
Hardy
Lake Road
2
4 K
Hardy
Lake
169
Torrance Road
N
Southwood Road
Muskoka Road 13
23.6 K
Lake
Muskoka
169
Circle Tour:
Lake Muskoka A
Muskoka Road 41
Bethune Drive
11
GRAVENHURST
1

CHAPTER 2

Circle Tour: Lake Muskoka (A)

Gravenhurst, Bala, Glen Orchard
Distance: 43 kilometres (27 miles)

S tarting at the Gateway to Gravenhurst, this tour takes you up the west side of Lake Muskoka to Bala and Glen Orchard. You'll travel around historic Muskoka Bay, once a booming sawmill and boatbuilding centre, as well as the headquarters for the Muskoka Navigation Company and its fleet of steamboats. The sole survivor of that fleet, the R.M.S. *Segwun*, in her crisp white and green livery, accents the waterfront scene. Farther along the route, the tour passes through Bala, a town built around cascading waterfalls. The *pièce de résistance* in late autumn is a trip to the cranberry marsh to watch the Johnston family harvest and package the bouncy red berries, which they claim are so fresh "they'll make your turkey blush."

The following chapter completes the circle tour of Lake Muskoka by commencing at Port Carling and travelling south to Bracebridge.

— Attractions —

Bethune House
235 John Street
Gravenhurst
705-687-4261

R.M.S. *Segwun*
Muskoka Bay
Gravenhurst
705-687-6667

Opera House and Arts Centre
Gravenhurst
705-687-5550 (box office)

Bala's Museum with
Memories of Lucy Maud Montgomery
Maple and River Street
Bala
705-762-5876

Johnston's Cranberry Marsh
Muskoka Road 169
705-762-3203
October only

1   GRAVENHURST

In many respects Gravenhurst is the Dawson City of Muskoka, although the "gold" was found above the ground, not below it. The gold came in the form of mature pine trees, which grew straight, thick and tall — in some cases up to 38 metres (125 feet). The logging fever hoisted the town from a moonscape of stumps and charred hillsides where settlers had used fire to help clear the land. Seymour Penson, a lithographer and early settler in Muskoka, spoke of the "denuded" landscape in Gravenhurst and the "desolation that follows the lumbermen."

Known by the locals as McCabe's Landing (after the first settler, James McCabe), the community gained official recognition when the settlers applied for a post office in 1862. An official with the Post Office Department, W.D. Lesueur, turned down the suggested name, McCabe's Landing, and substituted Gravenhurst, which came from a book he was reading at the time. Perhaps he

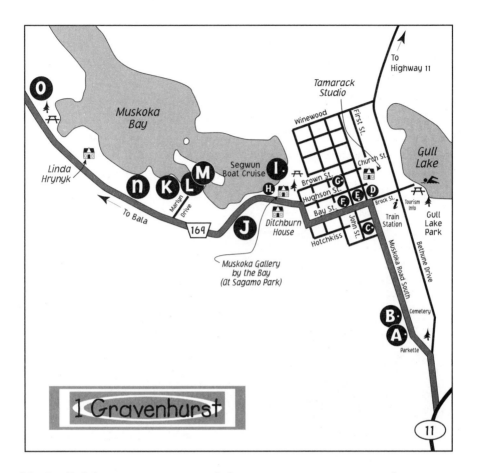

To
Highway 11

Tamarack
Studio

Winewood

First St.

Muskoka
Bay

Gull
Lake

Church St.

O

Linda
Hrynyk

Segwun
Boat Cruise

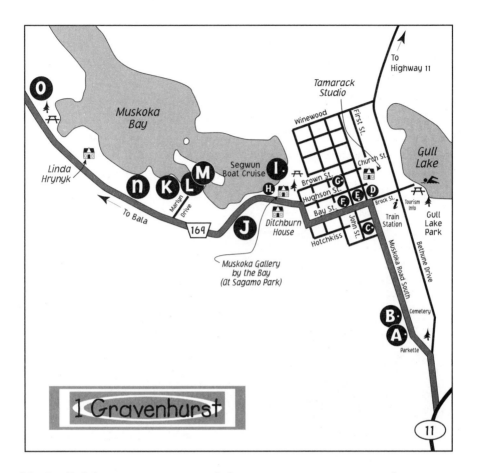

I.

Brown St.

G.

To Bala

Marlyn Drive

n K L M

H.

Hughson St.

F F D

Brock St.

i
Tourism
Info

Gull
Lake
Park

Bay St.

John St.

Train
Station

169

J

Ditchburn
House

C.

Muskoka Gallery
by the Bay
(at Sagamo Park)

Hotchkiss

Muskoka Road South

Bethune Drive

B·

Cemetery

A

Parkette

1 Gravenhurst

11

felt the fledgling community needed a more auspicious name if it were to become a success.

If success is measured in board feet of lumber, then Gravenhurst was indeed a gold mine for investors. Many sawmills operated in the area, most crowding the shores of Muskoka Bay, which was so full of saw logs that you could walk across it. Gravenhurst owed its good fortune not only to the arrival of the railway in 1875, but to its failure to "push on" to other centres farther north. For a decade Gravenhurst was the rail terminus in Muskoka. During that period most of Muskoka's felled timber made its way to Muskoka Bay in Gravenhurst to be processed for shipping. In one year alone, 30 million feet of lumber, plus 35 million shingles, left Gravenhurst, not counting the 50 million feet of logs and square timber. Gravenhurst was known as the Sawdust City of Muskoka.

For a town whose economy was dovetailed to the lumber business, it is not surprising to find the exclusive use of wood as an early building material.

For Gravenhurst that spelled disaster in 1887 when a fire originating in a foundry raced through the streets and destroyed everything. A newspaper article said: "The fire swept like a hurricane down Muskoka Street, carrying everything before it ... Not a business ... or hotel is left standing."

The pretty Victorian town you see now reflects the concern of the citizens to rebuild properly and on a more permanent basis. Today Gravenhurst bills itself as the first town in Muskoka. The slogan is correct on two counts; not only is the community the first town you reach when you travel into Muskoka, but the first to achieve town status, in 1887, at the height of the logging boom.

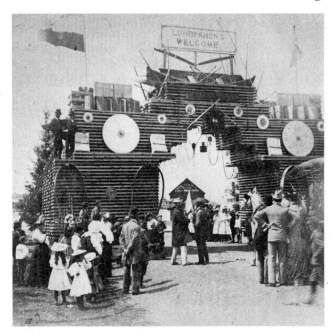

Gateway to Gravenhurst. Built by the Mickle-Dyment Company to welcome the Governor General on his visit to Muskoka.
PHOTO COURTESY
GRAVENHURST ARCHIVES

1A GATEWAY TO GRAVENHURST

Historian Frankie McArthur estimated there were five gateways erected in Gravenhurst over the years, not all in the same spot as this. The first gate was an arch of pine boughs to welcome Lord and Lady Dufferin when they passed this way in 1874. In 1885 the town again draped itself in pine boughs to honour the Governor General, the Fifth Marquis of Landsdowne. That year the Mickle-Dyment lumber company put up the lumberman's arch, a wooden structure bedecked with circular saws, crosscut saws, axes, pike poles and a rowboat. As years went by, the Gravenhurst Board of Trade erected other arches depicting Gravenhurst as the Gateway to Muskoka, the springboard for lakeland vacation and recreational adventure. The present gateway, erected in 1991, is a replica of the 1925 landmark.

1B JAMES MCCABE'S TAVERN SITE

Although no trace of it remains, McCabe's Tavern used to occupy the lot across the road from the cemetery. For many settlers the sight of Freemason's Arms Hotel was a welcome relief after the foreboding rocks and charred clearings along the Muskoka Road. Here at last was civilization. Or was it? The humble log structure "hunched" rather than "sat" on its foundation. Inside, Mother McCabe stirred up a thirst-quenching drink of vinegar, water and molasses — using her hand to mix the ingredients! The one-room structure was dining room, kitchen, living room and sleeping quarters for everyone, including the guests. In 1862 they added a post office to the menagerie of services in the one-room hotel. Most travellers, however, were thankful for the roof over their heads and had kind words to say about the McCabes' generosity

Prior to building the Freemason's Arms in 1861, the Irish couple had settled on Muskoka Bay, where they'd built a wharf; hence Gravenhurst's early name, McCabe's Landing.

1C THE OPERA HOUSE

When a fire destroyed the Gravenhurst town hall in 1897, council members decided it was time to erect a more substantial building, one befitting the town's status as an up-and-coming community. They employed a Toronto architect to design the building and spared no expense in outfitting it with chandeliers ($50 each) and a Heintzman piano ($300). The grand opening took place on March 12, 1901, with local notables taking part in recitations, songs and dancing.

With its spire, tower and keyhole windows, the opera house is both imposing and fanciful — like a gingerbread castle.

The much-loved building has been saved by the townspeople twice: once in 1965 when there was talk of replacing it with an all-purpose concrete edifice, and again in 1993 when the Province of Ontario closed the building for safety reasons. Officials worried the wooden arches would not hold the snow load.

The arches were replaced, the stage extended and a barrier-free entrance installed as part of a $2.7 million restoration. It re-opened in February 1995. The Gravenhurst Opera House and Arts Centre is one of only four Victorian period theatres in Ontario.

1D THE ALBION HOTEL

The original Albion Hotel, built in 1879 by G.W. Taylor, burned in the great fire of 1887. The present structure, with its attractive brickwork, was erected after the fire. In the late 1980s, the Town of Gravenhurst embarked on a restoration project to preserve the building as an example of Edwardian architecture.

Intersection of Muskoka Road and Bay Street, Gravenhurst,
showing the post office (right) and the Albion Hotel. PHOTO COURTESY IAN TURNBULL

1E THE POST OFFICE

The history of the northwest corner of Muskoka Road and Bay Street is a complex one. Beginning with Dugald Brown's Steamboat and Stage Hotel in 1867, there was a succession of ill-fated hostelries that changed hands several times and finally burned.

Meanwhile the post office location flitted about town, opening first in McCabe's Freemason's Arms, then in the Cockburn store, kitty-corner to the present post office location. In 1926 the government built the first storey of the new building, adding the second storey 1931. The building has been given historic classification by the Department of Public Works.

1F BROWN'S BEVERAGES

Just about everyone in Gravenhurst has a story to tell about Brown's Beverages. They may have worked at the plant as teenagers, or stood outside the James Street window as kids, watching the bottles being filled by the big machines inside. Up until 1988, Brown's Beverages was the oldest family-owned soft drink company in North America. Four generations of Browns ran the business. Dugald Brown established the industry in 1873 on Hotchkiss Street (a block south). Dugald died young, but his son J.D. Brown carried on the business and built a factory on Bay Street in the 1880s. J.D.'s son Leonard (Buster) Brown sold the company to Bill Snider.

Good water was the key to Brown's success in the early days. The family tapped into an artesian well, near the high school, and pumped the water to their Bay Street plant. People who lived along the route had water piped into their homes. These lines became the basis of Gravenhurst's present water system.

Dugald Brown had five original flavours: sarsaparilla, lemon, strawberry, gingerbeer and the famous Muskoka Dry gingerale, which is actually older than Canada Dry.

The original soft drink equipment was operated by a horse walking in a circle. Workers washed each pop bottle by hand, using a brush and lead pellets. Today Brown's Beverages is a distributor for Coca-Cola, Schweppes and the original Muskoka Dry. The recipe for the gingerale is still a closely guarded secret.

1G BETHUNE MEMORIAL HOUSE

It's worth straying from the Bay Street route to see this restored period home. The frame building, painted a cheery yellow, is the birthplace of Dr. Norman Bethune, a hero to the Chinese for his efforts in front-line medical care during the Japanese invasion of China.

Bethune House reproduces life as it was in the Victorian era, with luxuriant wallpaper, old-time gadgets and an organ with mouse-proof pedals. During the Christmas season, the staff holds an open house and serves traditional refreshments for visitors. Each summer there are special events planned in keeping with the historical setting.

— Norman Bethune—

The son of a Presbyterian minister, Norman Bethune spent his first years of an eventful life in the Gravenhurst manse. Later he studied medicine at the University of Toronto and served as a stretcher-bearer during the First World War. After the war Bethune developed tuberculosis and returned to Gravenhurst for a short time as a patient at the Calydor Sanatorium. Soon afterwards he was transferred to the Trudeau Sanatorium, in Saranac Lake. While suffering from the disease, Bethune pioneered a technique to combat it, and he went on to become a notable thoracic surgeon.

Joining the socialist cause, Bethune hurled himself into Spanish Civil War in the 1930s. On this mission he instigated the first mobile blood transfusion unit. Later he went to China and set up field hospital units during that country's war with Japan.

Bethune died helping the Chinese. Today his birthplace is a mecca for Chinese visitors, who have immortalized Bethune as a national hero.

1H SAGAMO PARK AND INTERPRETIVE CENTRE

Sagamo Park is named after the flagship of the Muskoka Navigation Company. The *Sagamo*, meaning "Big Chief," was built as a palace steamer — the biggest and most lavishly appointed steamer in the line.

The pretty park setting is not reminiscent of "the good old days" but an attempt to clean up the debris of commercial years. When the Muskoka Navigation Company operated a shipyard on this site, the area was littered with down-at-the-heel boathouses, docks and storage sheds, along with the usual piles of discarded lumber and machinery. In the heyday of lumbering (1860s to 1920s) the situation was worse still. Stockpiles of lumber and shingles cluttered the foreshore and the bay itself was clogged with saw logs and sawdust. Most of the sawmills operated around the Muskoka bay shoreline, blocking the view of the hillsides with their rickety wooden superstructures and jackladder devices. Not a pretty sight.

Today the scene is changing. Sagamo Park, officially opened in 1986, is the first step in beautifying the historic waterfront. The clipped lawns and neat walkways provide a pleasant backdrop for the majestic steamer *Segwun*, the *Sagamo's* sister ship and sole survivor of the Muskoka Navigation Company fleet.

The *Segwun's* ticket office and interpretive centre recreates the original Muskoka Wharf station (see 1K below). Here you can see a real steam engine in operation, or toot the whistles of old steamboats.

In addition, the Muskoka Steamship and Historical Society operates the *Wanda III*, a 94-foot steam launch built for Mrs. Margaret Eaton, wife of department store magnate, Timothy Eaton. Built in 1915, the *Wanda III* was the fastest steam yacht on the Muskoka lakes. Mrs. Eaton sold the yacht to C.O. Shaw for use as a hotel boat at Bigwin Inn, Lake of Bays. After acquiring the yacht in 1993, the Muskoka Steamboat and Historical Society spent $700,000 refurbishing it. The *Wanda III* began cruising the Muskoka lakes on charter trips in 1996.

R.M.S. Segwun.
PHOTO COURTESY FRED SCHULZ

1-I THE R.M.S. *Segwun*

Polished brass, a whiff of smoke and the slap of waves on the hull. For steam enthusiasts and romantics of all sorts, it's a dream come true — a ride on the Royal Mail Ship *Segwun*, one of the last coal-fired steamboats in North America. (The *Wanda III* is also steam-powered.)

The *Segwun* began her career in 1887 as the flagship of the Muskoka Navigation Company under her original name, *Nipissing II*. She was the first iron-hulled steamboat to ply the inland waterways of Ontario.

After remodelling the ship in 1925, the Navigation Company renamed her *Segwun*, an Ojibway word meaning "springtime." She still retains her Royal Mail Ship insignia. Any letters mailed aboard are franked with the *Segwun's* postmark and sent on their way at the next port.

When the Navigation Company pulled the last steamers off the lakes in the late 1950s, the *Segwun* eked out an existence as a floating museum. Today the *Segwun* is back in business as a result of a $1.2 million restoration project.

There's space to ramble and explore while the ship cruises by Muskoka shorelines. The engine room, gleaming with brass levers and dials, is open to public inspection. Through the grids on the deck floor you can watch crewmen scraping coal into the furnace.

Affectionately referred to as the "Love Boat" by Navigation Company manager Russ Brown, the *Segwun* is perhaps the most romantic spot in Muskoka for an evening meal. The Royal Muskoka Salon is circled with a bank of windows that brings you as close to the sunset as you can possibly get.

1J GREAVETTE BOATWORKS

The highway now runs over the site of the Greavette Boatworks, whose founder, Tom Greavette, was one of the first boat manufacturers in Muskoka to try assembly-line boatbuilding. He aimed to build a boat a day on each production line at his Gravenhurst plant, starting in 1931. When that didn't pan out, he turned to custom-designed boats.

Greavette learned his craft from the grandfather of Muskoka boatbuilding, Henry Ditchburn, at the Ditchburn plant nearby. Greavette left Ditchburn's employ and started his own enterprise, backed with money from former Ditchburn customers. The Depression hindered start-up procedures and shifted the emphasis of the business from mass production of stock boats to custom-built designs.

Built for speed and beauty, the Streamliner became one of Tom Greavette's best known models. As well, Greavette's *Little Miss Canada* and *Miss Canada*, built for Muskoka's racing legend Harold Wilson, captured national and international attention in the 1930s.

— Alexander Cockburn —
The Father of Muskoka

Muskoka owes much to the founder of the Muskoka Navigation Company, Alexander P. Cockburn. Without his vision and persistence, Muskoka could have had a much different story to tell.

In 1865, when he was the Reeve of Eldon Township in Victoria County, Cockburn took a trip to Muskoka and liked what he saw. In conversations with Darcy McGee, a minister in the pre-confederation government, Cockburn said he'd put a steamer on the lakes to encourage settlement if the government would undertake to open a navigation link between the three Muskoka lakes in the form of a lock at Port Carling (to join Lake Muskoka and Lake Rosseau) and a canal at Port Sandfield (linking Lake Rosseau and Lake Joseph).

Cockburn was so convinced of the future possibilities of the area that he went ahead with the launching of his steamboat, the *Wenonah*, in 1866 without receiving definite promises from government officials.

When the officials did come to take a look at the proposed sites for a lock and canal, Cockburn acted as their escort and shared his visions of a profitable navigation system opening up the country. For two decades Cockburn represented the political interests of Muskoka, first as a member of the provincial legislature, then in the House of Commons.

With the waterways open in 1871–72, Cockburn began expanding his fleet and writing tourist pamphlets which extolled the beauty of Muskoka. Cockburn's steamboat service made possible the development of luxury wilderness resorts like Rosseau House, which most people thought was a far-fetched idea at the time. The originator of the project, Mr. W. H. Pratt, had a suspicion that people would indeed pay to travel to the middle of nowhere if they were wined and dined in style once they got there. The idea caught on and soon there were similar resorts all around the lakes.

Having founded a navigation system and set the stage for tourism, Cockburn next turned his attention to getting the railway to Muskoka. Financially, it was a long, hard struggle to squeeze the necessary capital from local politicians and investors. Throughout it all, Cockburn remained optimistic and encouraging, and helped keep the project alive.

When A. P. Cockburn died in 1905, his navigation company was the largest of its kind in the country. As he had hoped, the steamboats encouraged settlement and stimulated business ventures. What's more, they established Muskoka's reputation as a premier holiday destination. For these reasons, the extraordinary A.P. Cockburn is accorded the title "The Father of Muskoka."

During the war years the Greavette operation built boats for the Air Force in its Gravenhurst plant and made parts for Fairmile patrol boats in Toronto. Tom Greavette died in 1958 and ownership of the company passed to Bruce Wilson, who moved the plant to Port Carling in 1978. The building was torn down in 1987.

To see what remains of the fabled Muskoka Wharf, the most important rail and steamboat depot in Muskoka's early history, turn right at Marlyn Drive and drive past the Silvaplex plywood plant.

1K MUSKOKA WHARF

These days there's not much to see at the once famous Muskoka Wharf, which is now in the clutches of some ghastly metal boathouses. But think what it was like here at the turn of the century. To your right, as you look out at the water, stood a pretty little station house (just like the one they've recreated at Sagamo Park). The tracks ran down the middle of the wharf. The hiss of the resting locomotives mixed with the creak of the steamers as they rubbed against the wharf. Hundreds of passengers jammed the landing at departure time. Children elbowed through the crowd to the dockside. Their mothers tracked them down while their fathers rounded up the luggage. Deck hands patiently sorted through the mountain of mail bags, steamer trunks, building material and groceries. Somehow they managed to get every item to its proper place and the steamers pulled away.

Muskoka Wharf as it used to be. You have to search diligently to find this site today on a backlot of a plywood manufacturing company. ONTARIO ARCHIVES S13013

1L RESTING PLACE OF THE SAGAMO STEAMER

Between the wharf and the ridge of rock to the right, you'll notice a pile of concrete rubble along the shoreline. Under that rubble is the rusted hull of the steamer *Sagamo*, towed here after its superstructure burned in 1969.

At that time it had been out of active service for a decade. It served for a short time as a floating restaurant to complement the *Segwun*, which had become a floating museum. After the fire the remains of the *Sagamo* were returned to this location, the spot where the steamer had been launched in 1906.

1M DITCHBURN BOAT MANUFACTURING COMPANY

The Muskoka Wharf area, as you have gathered, ranks high on the list of the most desolate spots in Muskoka, for it is here that so many early landmarks lie forgotten. The Muskoka Wharf is stripped of its prestige and put to mundane use; the *Sagamo*, the pride of the fleet, is buried unceremoniously beneath a heap of rubble; and the Ditchburn boatworks looks as forlorn as a month-old jack-o'-lantern. By the time you read this, in fact, the building may have been demolished altogether.

Henry Ditchburn, the founder of the boatworks, hailed from the Rosseau area, where he and his brothers settled in 1869. Encouraged by Mr. Pratt, the flamboyant proprietor of Rosseau House, the brothers built a fleet of fine rowboats and canoes for the tourists. After the Rosseau House burned in 1883, Henry organized a boatbuilding and rental business, operating from a shop near the Rosseau wharf.

By 1890 the Ditchburns had moved their headquarters to Gravenhurst. Their spot was ideally situated next to the busiest port of call on the Muskoka waterways at that time. The brick building, now painted yellow, was the second Ditchburn plant. The first building burned in 1915. Control of the company passed to Henry's nephew, Herbert, who continued to establish branch operations throughout Muskoka. Profits rolled in as the company crafted luxury yachts like the *Kawandag* — built for Sir John Eaton in 1916 — and the *Idlize* for Col. T. Duff.

Just before the Depression, Herbert Ditchburn began a major expansion project and invested heavily. The stock market crash ruined his plans and spelled the end of the Gravenhurst operation.

1N MICKLETOWN

The land where the Silvaplex buildings are located has been reclaimed from the original shoreline by years of sawdust accumulation from the sawmills that ringed the bay.

The Mickle, Dyment and Son lumber company operated sawmills in Severn Bridge and Gravenhurst.

The largest of the sawmills was the Mickle-Dyment Company, whose second mill was located here (Bayside Point Sales Office). As most of the mill hands lived close by, the area became known as Mickletown.

Charles Mickle founded the operation and later joined forces with Nathaniel Dyment. At its height the company operated mills at Bradford, Barrie, Fenelon Falls and Severn Bridge. The Mickle-Dyment mill outlived all other operations in Gravenhurst, but finally shut down in 1936.

1-O WEST GRAVENHURST

In the lumbering era, the big mills dominated the shoreline from Muskoka Wharf all the way to Hill Street. Stacked two to three storeys high, the piles of freshly cut wood actually looked like houses, hundreds of them, built shoulder to shoulder like tract housing.

Snaking between the piles of lumber were about 32 kilometres (20 miles) of railway track, counting the sidings and the main lines together. You can still spot the embankment of the old rail bed on the right hand side of the road as you travel north. To get to West Gravenhurst from Gravenhurst you had to work your way through the maze of lumber on a road made of wood shavings. Just about every day there would be a fire somewhere in the yard. The mills burned their refuse in a large burner which lit the sky at night. Some of the sawdust accumulated along the shore and built up into a "bridge" that was strong enough to hold a horse, if the rider didn't mind a spongy ride.

Charles Mickle's first lumber mill was located just north of the West Gravenhurst Park, where the lake comes close to the shore. The Snider Mill was situated behind the present-day Jug City, on Hill Street. G.W. Taylor built the mill and ran it until 1890. The Snider Company operated it until 1908.

When the old West Gravenhurst school (later used as a community hall) was scheduled for demolition, a group of volunteers saved the bell, which is now part of a memorial at the park. The school stood beside the Musquash Road, on a hill above the West Gravenhurst Park.

2   HARDY LAKE PARK

You can't help but use superlatives in describing Hardy Lake. It is one of the prettiest little lakes in south Muskoka — and there is not a house or cottage on it. Along the west shore, there's a thin strip of white sand that looks like it's been flown in from the Pacific Ocean. In the same vicinity you'll find the ruins of an old homestead. The stone foundation is a marvel of pioneer architecture, still solid and sturdy enough to build on.

Hardy Lake Park includes 648 hectares (1,600 acres) of land around Hardy Lake and 6,480 metres (four miles) of shoreline on Lake Muskoka. Near the northwest corner of the lake a rare aquatics zone features aquatic plants that are normally found along the Atlantic coast. Another section of the park contains an open bog and black spruce/larch forest that supports a number of rare orchids and two species of rare insects.

In all, it's a naturally and historically significant place that you are welcome to explore *for the day*. The Province of Ontario has no immediate plans to add visitor facilities such as toilets, campgrounds or access roads. The only way in is by foot or canoe. There's room to park two cars where the lake comes close to Muskoka Road 169. Walkers are better off to take Torrance Road to East Bay Road. Just past Camp Crossroads you will see Hardy Lake Road. At the end of the gravel road, you can park your car and follow the trail to the old homestead site.

3   BALA "THE CRANBERRY CAPITAL OF ONTARIO"

Come October, the citizens of Bala pull out their kettles and pans and begin cooking up batches of cranberry muffins, cranberry breads, cranberry pies and cranberry chutneys. Anything that can be made with cranberries, is cooked up in huge quantities for the Cranberry Festival, held the weekend after Thanksgiving. The only commercial cranberry operations in Ontario are centred around Bala, making it the official Cranberry Capital of Ontario. Over 17,000 people converge on the town to help them celebrate the cranberry harvest.

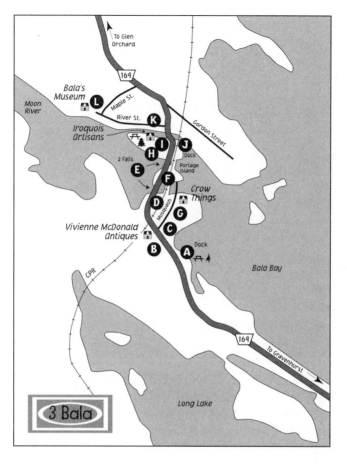

The community of Bala grew up on a small island set between the Mill Stream and the falls. With the amount of water rushing by, you'd wonder how a town could ever get a toehold in this precarious position. Now that it has, it's blessed with the refreshing sound of falling water.

Scottish-born Thomas Burgess named the community after the Bala lake district in Wales. He arrived in 1868 and set up a sawmill on the north channel, since called the Mill Stream. Almost single-handedly Burgess created a community. In addition to the sawmill he ran a general store, a bake shop, a blacksmith shop and a supply boat. He applied for a post office in 1872. That same year contractors pushed the Musquash Road through from Gravenhurst. The railway followed in 1907.

Bala is unique in being the only community in Muskoka to jump from township rule to town status without first serving a "municipal apprenticeship" as a village. Bala was incorporated as a town in 1914 and for years has prided itself as being the smallest town in Canada.

Bala's CPR summer station. It was a hectic place on Friday night when the "Daddy train" arrived, bringing husbands up to be with their families. PHOTO COURTESY OF LORNE JEWITT

3A WINDSOR PARK

Windsor Park takes its name from a large, three-storeyed hotel that occupied the site in the early days. If you look carefully, you can see the raised rectangular plot where the foundations of the New Windsor Hotel sat. The park is also the site of Bala's second hotel, the Clifton House, built in 1890 by John Board. (The first hotel was Bala Falls).The Boards sold Clifton House to William McDivitt in 1900. He had been operating the Windsor Hotel in Gravenhurst and took on the Clifton House in an effort to expand the family enterprise.

The McDivitts changed the name of the small boarding house to Windsor Hotel and proceeded to add several annexes to the existing structure, along with a laundry and gas house. The building burned in June 1907.

From the ashes of the Windsor came the New Windsor Hotel. The McDivitts operated the resort well into the 1940s. After the building left their hands, it changed owners several times and was finally demolished in 1969.

3B BALA BAY INN (SWASTIKA HOTEL)

E.B. Sutton built Muskoka's first brick summer resort. The guest registers at the hotel date back to 1912, and it's possible the hotel opened even earlier. Sutton called the resort the Swastika Hotel, incorporating the ancient symbol for peace on a sign above the balcony. When the Nazis adopted the same symbol, the Suttons changed the hotel name to Sutton Manor. Later the name changed to Bala Bay Lodge and Bala Bay Inn. You can still make out the swastika on a plate above the balcony of the inn.

Bala street scene in the 1920s, showing (left to right) the frame church, the Royal Bank (now the post office) and the J.W. Burgess store (now Portage Landing). PHOTO COURTESY OF LORNE JEWITT

Ephraim Browning Sutton, the founder of the hotel, moved into Bala from Medora Township in 1899 to open a general store. He wrote a lively newspaper column in which he expressed strong opinions about many issues, including water quality. A talented musician and lyricist, Sutton wrote such songs as "Give Me a Song That's Gay" and "Lovely Lake Muskoka." He'd also met novelist Charles Dickens and wrote to him on several occasions. When E.B. Sutton died, his son Fred took charge of the resort.

3C INTERSECTION OF MUSKOKA ROAD 169 AND MUSQUASH ROAD

This intersection marks the juncture of two routes into town. Musquash Road is the original main street. It takes you past Dunn's dance pavilion, the cenotaph, Trinity St. Alban's Church and Burgess Memorial Church.

The newer route into town passes an archaeological point of interest, a striking rock cut that was blasted in the mid-1960s when the bypass road went in.

3D ARCHAEOLOGICAL PLAQUE

The best parking area for viewing the falls is in front of the rock cut. Had you been standing here before 1964, you'd have been underwater. Contractors blasted the rock and built the new road on reclaimed land to allow transport trucks access through Bala. The trucks could not squeeze through the underpass on Musquash Road.

The rock cut is highlighted by an archaeological plaque describing the Precambrian Shield. According to some geologists, the plaque is a bit misleading because it describes the Shield in general terms rather than in ways that relate to Muskoka. The allusion to mineral wealth, for example, does not apply in this district.

Still, you get a good view of the folds in the rock, which are outlined by lines of dark amphibolite in sugary pink gneiss (pronounced "nice"). Gneiss is a metamorphic rock composed of feldspar, quartz and mica. It is distinguished by banding patterns that give it a layered look. Most of the rock in Muskoka is gneiss, although laymen mistakenly confuse it with granite.

3E BALA FALLS

Viewing the falls in Bala never fails to stir emotion. All the water from Algonquin Park and the three big Muskoka lakes flows through here on its way to Georgian Bay. Downstream the river branches into the Moon and the Musquash rivers.

There are actually two sets of falls in Bala: the main outlet, which cascades past the town park, and the spillway, which plummets through a narrow gap behind Burgess Memorial Church.

Before the Department of Public Works installed a dam on the main outlet in 1873, water levels on Lake Muskoka went up and down like a yo-yo. But the first dam kept water levels too high and farmers complained that their fields were being inundated. As a result, the department began blasting out spillways on the south channel, which, in its natural state, had not carried that much water. By 1878 the blasting of spillways had deepened the south channel so much that a dam was called for, and one was installed that year.

3F BURGESS MEMORIAL CHURCH, PORTAGE ISLAND

Portage Island is cut up like a pie by the roads and railway, but it retains some of its earlier charm as the setting for Burgess Memorial Church. Built of pleasing Muskoka stone, the building is a picturesque place of worship.

Die-hard Presbyterians built the church in 1926 after splitting from their former congregation, which had accepted church union of the Methodist and Presbyterian faiths. A plaque near the entrance indicates that the church was built in memory of Bala's founder Thomas W. Burgess.

3G THE KEE TO BALA

For the baby-boomer generation, The Kee was an inescapable part of Muskoka summers. Every back road had The Kee's flyers posted on fence post or maple trees — bright bold announcements of coming engagements. The Kee's stadium-sized dance floor was always packed, shoulder to shoulder, with swaying bodies.

Gerry Dunn created the big pavilion for another era, the Big Band Era. The late Hugh Clairmont, a local jazz musician, said it personified a charming period in time: "The bandstand resembled the front of a cottage, with its white exterior and its windows, awnings and all, being decorated by flower boxes and a palm tree, no less. On warm nights, the dancers could cool off on a huge outdoor balcony overlooking Bala Bay and view the star-filled sky and the moon peeking through nearby mammoth pine trees."

Pharmacist Gerry Dunn opened his first open-air pavilion in Bala in 1929. It was part of his ice cream parlour and general store business. As the popularity of the dance hall grew, he expanded, tearing down the old pavilion and opening the building now known as The Kee on July 1, 1942.

To this idyllic, out-of-the-way location, Dunn managed to entice most of the big-name bands of the day: Guy Lombardo, Woody Herman, Stan Kenton, Duke Ellington, Les Brown and his Band of Renown, the Dorsey Brothers.

Gerry Dunn decided to get out of the dance hall business in 1962, but the pavilion has rightly earned its place as a Muskoka landmark. Times change, the music changes, but the magic of the pavilion is as it always was, and that is best summed up in the words of a summer cottager of the 1940s who said: "When you're really in the mood to have fun, going over to Dunn's is great. It makes you want to pick up a nice pretty girl and whirl her away onto the dance floor, and care for nothing save her loveliness and the whirling, swinging, leaping vigour of dancing."

3H FOUNDING OF BALA (Historic Marker)

A marker highlighting the early history of Bala is found in the park on the north side of the falls. This area has a cathedral-like atmosphere, with tall pines and oak trees forming a vaulted canopy overhead.

Carr's Ice Cream Parlour and Dance Pavilion took advantage of the falls location here with verandahs that hung out over the water. The building was situated next to the roadway.

3-I PORTAGE LANDING

Portage Landing is the original J.W. Burgess store, built in 1907 by Thomas Burgess's son. His father's store stood across the street and had to be removed when the railway came to town. The Davidson family renovated the store in 1997, creating retail space that's very much in keeping with Bala's home-town atmosphere.

The post office, beside Portage Landing, was originally the Royal Bank. The United church dates back to the 1930s. It replaced the Presbyterian church built on land donated by Thomas Burgess in 1893. The first church burned in 1934.

The parking lot across from the store was once a town park with clipped hedges, trimmed lawns and a water fountain.

3J   THE CPR RAILWAY STATION

The Canadian Pacific Railway reached Bala in 1907, crossing overland from Severn Falls. No trace of the station buildings remains to remind us of the hustle and bustle of those early days; days when hundreds of passengers disembarked from the trains and boarded steamboats to destinations around the lake. The tracks were laid at the top of an incline that dropped steeply to Lake Muskoka. Builders constructed a platform to support the station building. A ramp and stairway led to the wharf at the lower level.

To get to the wharf today, you must go under the railway trestle at the south end of the parking lot. It's worth walking around that way, as the view of Bala Bay is quite striking.

3K   BALA HYDRO ELECTRIC DEVELOPMENT (Historic Marker)

On the banks of the Mill Stream, behind the office of Gidley Real Estate (at one time a Burgess bakery), there's a plaque commemorating the development of a hydroelectric scheme in 1917.

The generating station is built on the spot where Thomas Burgess had fashioned a timber dam and water wheel to run a sawmill. The sawmill operated on this site from 1870 until 1910. Members of the Burgess family helped found the Bala Electric Light and Power Company. It was taken over by Ontario Hydro in 1929.

In 1988–89 Marsh Hydropower Inc. leased the old powerhouse, which had been idle for many years, and got things going again. The small hydro development sells the power it produces to Ontario Hydro. The rejuvenated plant is called, fittingly, the Burgess Generating Station.

3L   BALA'S MUSEUM

The Anne of Green Gables books made author Lucy Maud Montgomery a legend in this country. Most of her novels are set in Prince Edward Island, but there is one that was inspired by the town of Bala. L.M. Montgomery stayed at Roselawn Lodge in 1922. A daydream on the porch of the inn led to the novel *The Blue Castle*. While in Bala for two weeks that July, the author took all her meals at the Tree Lawn Tourist Home, which has been lovingly restored as a museum by Jack and Linda Hutton. All of L.M. Montgomery's 22 books, including a first edition of *The Blue Castle*, are on display at the museum, which now houses one of the most extensive collections of the author's books in the world. Japanese visitors are so taken with the L.M. Montgomery memorabilia that they come here in droves. The Huttons have had to learn basic Japanese phrases. Bala's Museum is linked to a web site of a Tokyo museum that focuses on Anne of Green Gables.

4 JOHNSTON'S CRANBERRY MARSH
(October only)

They say you can tell a ripe cranberry by its bounce, and "bounciness" is at the heart of this cranberry operation. Like tiny red golf balls, the ripe berries bounce down an mechanical incline called the Hayden separator. To make the grade the berries must leap over all the hurdles set in their path. Only the fittest berries make it to the conveyor belt; those that don't, get dumped in the garbage.

This is a great place. Not only can you watch the cranberries competing in the separation "Olympics," but you can watch the little harvester churning round the marsh, combing the berries from the vines. In tow, behind the harvester, are tiny punts that collect the mountains of cranberries harvested each season.

Cranberries grow naturally in this environment, but the Johnstons are helping nature along. Orville Johnston developed the marsh in the early '50s. He cleared and irrigated the marshes and planted "Searle jumbo" cranberries, native to Eagle River, Wisconsin. The commercial operation began in 1953. Three years later the first crop was ready for harvesting.

To harvest the berries the Johnstons flood the marshes. The cranberries, still attached to their vines, pop to the surface, where they are combed gently from the vines by the harvester. The flooding of the marshes also helps protect the ripe berries from frost damage — although a nip of cold weather is needed to bring out the deep red colour we look for in cranberries.

The harvest takes place through October. The operation is open to the public during that time. The Johnstons also sell whole cranberries and other products, such as cranberry chutney and cranberry relish.

Note: To take a look at a different cranberry harvesting method, you can also visit the Iroquois Cranberry Growers just south of MacTier on Highway 69. The Iroquois Growers use a water reel to beat the berries from the flooded vines. The berries float to the surface, creating a ribbon of crimson on brilliant blue water.

5 GLEN ORCHARD
During a snow fall in November 1868, John Nixon and his wife Susan (Henshaw) struggled over a miserable trail from Port Carling to Glen Orchard.

At the crossing on the north end of Butterfly Lake the ox that had been pulling their cart fell off a makeshift bridge into the bog and it took them hours to get the animal and their possessions out of the muck. They finally made it to Ada Lake, and settled there. In two years' time Nixon's wife's relatives and friends (the Henshaws and the Orchards) joined him. The Henshaws settled at Henshaw Lake, which you pass on the way to Port Carling. Nathaniel Orchard built his home on the site of the Glen Orchard store.

Orchard's farmhouse became the hub of the community when he opened a post office there. As Orchard's home was situated in a glen between Ada Lake and Butterfly Lake, he chose the name Glen Orchard for the post office. At that time he walked to Gravenhurst once a week to collect the mail.

The early settlers soon discovered they could not survive as farmers in this rocky crossroads community. Their neighbours on the Muskoka lakes had tourism to fall back on. For landbound settlers the only alternative revenue came from the lumber industry. Fortunately, William Fairhall operated a substantial mill at nearby Whiteside, and it was here that many of the Glen Orchard men worked.

After you turn onto Muskoka Road 118, you'll notice the old frame schoolhouse on the Glen Orchard cemetery grounds on White's Road. It was built in 1890 and is now the Women's Institute hall.

6   MARY GROVE (Glen Home)

On July 29, 1939, Mr. Lambert Love held opening ceremonies for his new hotel, Glen Home. It was a stylish building with corner turrets built up in tiers like a wedding cake (the top tiers have since been removed).

Lambert Love had previously owned and operated Elgin House on the opposite shore. Much later in life, Lambert Love married again and had a second family. He left the management of Elgin House to his son Bert and moved his second family to Glen Home.

Love's years of experience in the tourism business are reflected in the layout of Glen Home, both in terms of making a pleasant environment for the guests and in creating an efficient work area for the staff. Of particular interest are screened-in balconies off every suite (a convenience not found in other resorts of that era).

Although some people thought a resort with "no drinking and no smoking" restrictions could not possibly survive, Lambert Love proved there was a demand for holiday destinations with a Christian atmosphere. A staunch Methodist in his religious views, Lambert Love insisted that all staff members attend chapel services at the resort. Any infringement of the moral code of the establishment meant instant dismissal, and minor infractions, such as falling asleep in church, led to severe reprimand in Love's office (often called the Lion's Den).

Lambert's wife Alice and son Paul continued to operate the resort after Lambert's death. Paul closed the resort on Labour Day 1974. When the resort came up for sale, the Sisters of St. Joseph, a Roman Catholic order, purchased it. The sisters, who've renamed the hotel Mary Grove, come up for vacations or retreats.

7 PINELANDS RESORT

An interesting thing about Pinelands Resort is that it is not the *original* Pinelands at all, but Belmont House. Pinelands House, now torn down, sat adjacent the Belmont and the two were run as one from 1942 onwards.

John and Elizabeth Jones moved their family to this spot in 1895, although they'd been in Muskoka since 1880, living in and around Port Sandfield. Jones worked as a porter at Prospect House, then established a hotel of his own in 1906. Pinelands House also became the post office for this section of the lake.

The rooms had a spartan simplicity in those days, with dark window shades and mattresses filled with straw. One guest remembers waking each morning to the sound of cow bells as the dairy herd came in for milking.

William Fairhall, a sawmiller from Lake Muskoka, purchased property adjacent Jones and began building Belmont House in 1902. The hotel opened in 1904. Perhaps his experience in the lumber business gave Fairhall an edge in designing buildings, for the Belmont House was, and still is, a very pleasing hotel to look at. There's something "complete" about the arrangement of the four towers and the second-storey sun porch. Certainly the Belmont had a lovely view over the beach — which just happens to be the prettiest stretch of sandy shoreline on Lake Joseph.

In 1942 Clarence and Bert Jones (John's sons) purchased the Belmont and operated the resorts as Pinelands Lodges. The Lydans bought the resorts in 1961 and sold to the Revilles in 1970. The Revilles found they had to tear the old Pinelands House down, as it had fallen into such a state of disrepair as to be dangerous.

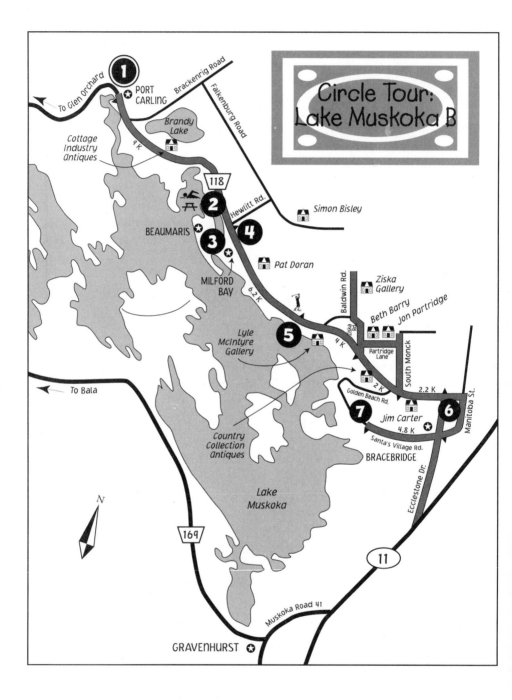

Circle Tour:
Lake Muskoka B

To Glen Orchard

1 PORT CARLING

Brackenrig Road

Falkenburg Road

Brandy Lake

Cottage Industry Antiques

9 K

118

2

Hewlitt Rd.

Simon Bisley

BEAUMARIS

3

4

Pat Doran

MILFORD BAY

6.2 K

Baldwin Rd.

Ziska Gallery

Ziska Rd.

Beth Barry

Jon Partridge

Lyle McIntyre Gallery

5

4 K

Partridge Lane

South Monck

To Bala

2 K

2.2 K

Manitoba St.

Golden Beach Rd.

7

Jim Carter

6

4.8 K

Country Collection Antiques

Santa's Village Rd.

BRACEBRIDGE

Ecclestone Dr.

Lake Muskoka

N

169

11

Muskoka Road 41

GRAVENHURST

CHAPTER 3

Circle Tour: Lake Muskoka (B)

Port Carling, Bracebridge
Distance: 27 kilometres (17 miles)

Port Carling is called the Hub of the Lakes, which is entirely appropriate given its location at the centre of the three big lakes. From here, the tour continues southeast along Muskoka Road 118, through the district's longest rock cut, to the town of Bracebridge, where you can take a historic tour of the falls.

The route passes by the studios of some of Muskoka's most talented artists and artisans. I call it the "Arts and Crafts" route because there are so many interesting shops to visit. These are the studios and galleries that have helped establish the reputation of the artists' colony in Muskoka. The studio tour concept, now popular throughout the province, originated in Muskoka. The Muskoka Autumn Studio Tour, held two weekends prior to Thanksgiving, gives visitors a tantalizing peek inside the artists' homes and a chance to see how their work is made.

Those studios mentioned here are ones I've visited and enjoyed. There are many more studios scattered throughout Muskoka. No doubt, you'll make discoveries of your own along the way.

— ATTRACTIONS —

Muskoka Lakes Museum
Island Park
Port Carling
705-765-5367

Lady Muskoka
Ecclestone Drive
Bracebridge
705-646-2628

Santa's Village and Sportsland
Santa's Village Road
Bracebridge
705-645-2512

Woodchester Villa
King Street
Bracebridge
705-645-8111

Chapel Gallery
King Street
Bracebridge
705-645-5501
(Closed Mondays)

— SIGHTS —

Port Carling Locks
Huckleberry Rock Cut
Bracebridge Falls and park
Bird Mill Mews

— ANTIQUES —

Cottage Industry Antiques
and Country Design
Muskoka Road 118
Port Carling
705-764-0575

Country Collection
Muskoka Road 118
Bracebridge
705-645-9191

Wildflower Antiques
Manitoba Street
Bracebridge
705-646-8771

— ARTS AND CRAFTS —

Eidlitz Pottery and Paintbox
145 Medora Street
Port Carling
705-765-5167

Frank and Phoebe Roads
(Native crafts)
Indian Village
Port Carling
705-765-5173
June to Thanksgiving

The Muskoka Moose
Maple Street
Port Carling
705-765-7156

The Village Place
Joseph Street
Port Carling
705-765-5717

Simon Bisley Glass
Off Muskoka Road 118
(north on Hewlitt Road,
right on Falkenburg)
705-764-1376
Tuesday to Sunday

Pat Doran (handcrafted signs)
Muskoka Road 118
Milford Bay
705-764-8909

Lyle McIntyre's Muskoka
Harbour Gallery
Muskoka Road 118
at Cedar Beach Road
705-645-8814

Ziska Gallery
Off Muskoka Road 118
(north on Ziska Road)
705-645-2587

Jon Partridge Pottery
Off Muskoka Road 118
(north on South Monck Drive,
left on Partridge Lane)
705-645-8618
Wednesday to Saturday

Beth Barry Pottery
Off Muskoka Road 118
(north on South Monck Drive,
left on Partridge Lane)
705-645-9149

Jim Carter
(blacksmith and ironwork art)
Muskoka Road 118
Bracebridge
705-645-6569

Shards 'n' Shavings
Manitoba Street
Bracebridge
705-645-4531

Muskoka Pottery and Glass
Manitoba Street
Bracebridge
705-646-2460

Scott's of Muskoka
Manitoba Street
Bracebridge
705-645-5127

Bird Mill Gallery
At the falls
Bracebridge
705-645-413

1 PORT CARLING "THE HUB OF THE LAKES"

If you can conspire to be in Port Carling on Monday at noon during the
R.M.S. *Segwun's* sailing season, the town will etch itself forever in your
memory. That's when the restored steamboat heaves into view, announcing her
arrival with a throaty blast. At first there's nothing to see but a plume of steam
rising above the tree line. Then the *Segwun* rounds the corner of the Indian
River, looking as if she's just sailed off the cover of a book. The bridge tilts like
a ski jump, and the *Segwun* glides into the locks. For a moment you're engulfed
in a swirl of steam that smells of coal and engines; then the mists part and the
Segwun continues her journey, breaking the spell and jolting you back to the
1990s. This weekly return to the steamboat era befits a town that owes its
existence to the coming and going of the steamers.

Port Carling is actually Muskoka's oldest community. It started as an
Ojibway settlement. Surveyor Vernon Wadsworth found it well established in
1860 when he described a bustling community with 20 log huts and land

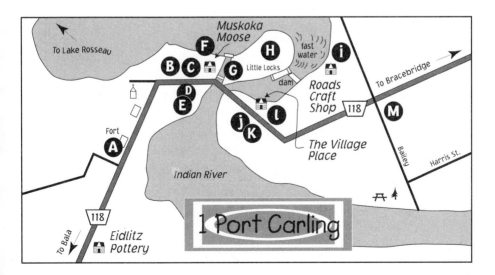

Port Carling in the 1890s, showing the bridge over the Indian River and the swing bridge. The roof of the Interlaken Hotel can be seen above the trees. MUSKOKA LAKES MUSEUM

cleared for the planting of corn and potatoes. The natives called their village Obajewanung, meaning "gathering place." New settlers often referred to the community as Indian Gardens. The Ojibway stayed in the village for some years before relocating on Parry Island, near Parry Sound.

Around 1865 the Bailey brothers arrived. Alexander claimed the land in the south end of the village and Michael settled on the north side of the river. That same year Donald Cockburn (brother to A. P. Cockburn of Navigation Company fame) arrived and started building a trading post at the site of the present locks. But it took the arrival of the eccentric Benjamin Hardcastle Johnston to get things moving in the town.

At that time the Baisong Rapids were a real bottleneck for navigation. The solution, of course, was to install a dam and a navigational lock, an idea helped along by Johnston, with the support of steamboat magnate A.P. Cockburn. Johnston had an ally in the government at that time: John Carling, the minister of Public Works. Carling's colleagues in the ministries of Roads and Crown Lands saw the project as a waste of money. They went so far as to liken its significance to linking up "two frog ponds." But Carling got the idea passed, on the grounds that such a navigational link would encourage settlement.

Work began on the lock in the spring of 1869. That same year, Johnston was appointed postmaster. He named the community Port Carling after John Carling. It wasn't until some years later, in June 1896, that Port Carling was incorporated as a village.

IA THE HANNA HOUSE AND JOHNSTON'S FORT

At the turn of the century Benjamin Hardcastle Johnston built this attractive red brick home (opposite the Muskoka Lakes Association office), which he sold to William Hanna, the owner of the Hanna Company general store. The Hanna family lived in it for 23 years. On the hill behind the house you'll notice the remains of Johnston's fort. The ruins are on private property, but are visible from the roadway, especially when the leaves are down in the autumn. Johnston built the fort to guard the village from Fenian attack. At that time the expatriate Irish Fenians were raiding English settlements along the Canadian/American border. William Hanna later built a water tank on the foundation of the fort.

Benjamin Hardcastle Johnston,
Port Carling's first postmaster.
MUSKOKA LAKES MUSEUM

IB STRATTON HOUSE

A pretty hotel called the Stratton House sat where the town parking lot is today. It burned in 1912, taking the old Anglican Church with it. At that time Gravenhurst had the nearest fire engine. They sent it up on a steamboat and it arrived in time to cool the ashes.

1C THE POLAR STAR (PORT CARLING HOUSE)

In 1871 Mr. John Thomas fixed up Michael Bailey's rough log boarding house on the north side of the lock and called it the Polar Star Hotel. After 17 years he sold the hotel to Robert Arksy. Arksy built the Interlaken Hotel around the original log structure. Later, he sold the business to Joseph Ruddy and Ruddy changed the name to Port Carling House. In later years, the building sat derelict. It was finally torn down in 1970. The purchasers of the property were hoping to build a new restaurant and condominium units but were unable to obtain planning approval. During the demolition of the building, the workmen uncovered the logs of the original boarding house, built by Michael Bailey back in 1869. Today a line of modern shops sits on what used to be the front lawn of the hotel.

1D HANNA'S STORE

In 1881 William Hanna moved to Port Carling and opened a small store. Prior to that he'd helped his father with the mails in Muskoka Falls and spent some time as a store clerk in Bracebridge. A newspaper article printed in the *Toronto World*, July 14, 1887, describes Hanna's operation as "a real bazaar" where a purchaser could find everything he desired. Hanna expanded his operation several times and in 1900 moved down the street to this location (former IGA building) beside the river.

As a sideline, Hanna ran two supply boats, the *Mink* and *Newminko*, which acted as floating stores. The supply boats were a boon to cottagers, who hoisted white flags on their docks if they wanted the steamers to call. When the boat arrived, crowds of customers clambered aboard. While the butcher chopped and dispensed cuts of meat in a hand-over-fist fashion, the clerk fielded transactions for cottage staples such as candles, coal oil and maple syrup.

In October 1931 a fire started in the basement of Hanna's store and spread up the main street. The fire occurred the day after the Port Carling Boatworks had burned to the ground. Together, the two fires virtually wiped out the town. By the following summer, however, the scars had healed. Port Carling merchants rebuilt, mostly in brick. The former IGA store is the building the Hannas put up at that time.

1E DUKE MARINE SERVICES

The Duke Marine Services building is a powerful reminder that Port Carling was, at one time, a boatbuilder's town. Everyone built boats. "There wasn't anything else to do in Port Carling," oldtimer Charlie Amey once remarked. For the most part the enterprises clustered on the shorelines above and below the locks. Names like Johnston, Matheson, SeaBird and Duke feature prominently in the boatbuilding history of the town.

Charlie Duke began boatbuilding in the Port Carling area as early as 1910, but it was not until 1924 that he and his partner, Ernie Greavette, established headquarters in this location. The partnership soon dissolved and Duke continued building launches and rowboats with his sons Claude and Aud. When the Hanna Store fire swept through town in 1931, workers tried saving the new hulls in the Duke shop by dropping them over the well into the boat slip ten feet below. Many survived their premature christening and became cherished launches on the lakes.

The Dukes rebuilt the shop after the fire and continued their successful business until 1977, when Ed Skinner and Rick Terry purchased the operation.

Preceding the Dukes' tenure, the site marked the location of John Matheson's boatworks. Matheson, a former employee of W.J. Johnston, set up

Duke Boats has been part of the waterfront scene since 1924.
The Twenty-One Club, beside it, was a popular night spot. <small>MUSKOKA LAKES MUSEUM</small>

a shop in direct competition with Johnston after the two men had an argument. Matheson, an Orkney Islander, ran away to sea at the age of 12. He came to Canada and set up a boatbuilding shop in Toronto. He moved to Muskoka to do some carpentry work on Chief's Island. He heard W.J. Johnston was looking for people to build boats and took him up on the offer. Matheson is acknowledged as one of the finest craftsman of his era.

1F PORT CARLING BOAT WORKS/ HUGH MACLENNAN AND SONS

When the Disappearing Propeller Boat Company folded (see below), W.J. Johnston Jr. started the Port Carling Boat Works. He brought along some of the employees of the DP company, including Cameron and Doug Milner, Charlie McCulley and Harold Cooper. They started making cedar lapstrake outboards, rowboats and a boat similar, but not identical, to the disappearing propeller boat. Then came the SeaBirds, a line of boats that established the company's reputation. Well built, but competitively priced, the SeaBirds put ownership of a motor launch within range of the average family.

In 1931 the boatworks burned completely, but by the mid-1930s had revived and expanded, setting up a companion operation in Honey Harbour. About that time a farmer named Hugh MacLennan came to Port Carling from Uffington to look for work at the Port Carling Boatworks. He eventually bought the company in 1965. Today the company is run by Hugh MacLennan Jr. and his wife Joan.

The locks at Port Carling. PHOTO BY G.W. CAMPBELL

1G PORT CARLING LOCKS

Port Carling is known as the Hub of the Lakes, "the place where the waters meet." This strategic position focused attention on the Baisong Rapids, a navigational bottleneck. In pioneer days the roads were either non-existent or in primitive condition. People like A.P. Cockburn were quick to realize that the future growth and development of Muskoka depended on an unimpeded flow of traffic on the Muskoka lakes. As Muskoka's representative in provincial government, he put forward a case for constructing a navigation lock at Port Carling.

You get an indication of the problems those early travellers faced when you discover that prior to the construction of the lock and the removal of shoals in the Indian River, steamboats could not get close enough to the shoreline to allow passengers to disembark in a civilized fashion. The *Wenonah* stopped some distance from shore and put out a gang plank. While a weighty member of the crew held down one end, passengers jumped ashore from the other. The cargo had to be portaged across to Lake Rosseau and reloaded in another craft.

Construction of the lock began in 1869, but difficulties with high water and blasting slowed things down. The lock opened for navigation in November 1871, and it's been expanded and rebuilt several times since then. One of the most welcome improvements was the installation of electric gates to speed up the procedure. Lockages that once took 30 minutes are now completed in ten.

Muskoka Lakes Museum. PHOTO BY G.W. CAMPBELL

Meanwhile, more and more pleasure craft were appearing on the lakes. Their coming and going taxed the large lock facility and upset the lake level by allowing too much water to pass through. For the convenience of these craft, the government installed the small lock in 1921. This was replaced in 1940 and automated in the 1960s.

1H THE MUSKOKA LAKES MUSEUM AND THE ISLAND

The island did not look as parklike as it does now. It was, in fact, covered in tall pine trees and ringed round the edges by a strange collection of boat liveries and sheds. Part of that collection was a corrugated-iron building called the fish hatchery, which stood not far from the present museum.

The Muskoka Lake Museum is a relative newcomer on the island, built during Canada's centennial year, 1967. Several wings have been added since that time, along with Hall House. This settler's home is a real beauty. You have to marvel at the size of the trees the pioneers had to work with. The logs in Hall House are 66 centimetres (26 inches) thick and nine metres (30 feet) long.

The log home recreates the life of Muskoka's early pioneers and is furnished with local artifacts. Throughout the operating season, the museum staff conduct workshops for visitors who may spend the day weaving baskets, dipping candles or gardening. Spinners and quilters make regular visits to the museum to demonstrate their craft. The Marine Room honours Port Carling's boatbuilding heritage. Several of the old boats are on display, including the renowned disappearing propeller boat.

The Muskoka Lake Museum houses one of the best collections of resort memorabilia and a comprehensive photographic file, proving, once again, that good things do come in small packages.

1I   INDIAN VILLAGE

As Port Carling was first known as Indian Village, it is fitting that an Indian village still exists in the town. The four-acre site (across the river from the museum) was a traditional campgrounds for the natives, who returned here from Parry Island or Rama each summer. Later, they were joined by Mohawks from the Wahta Reserve

With the influx of tourists, the natives found a steady market for their handcrafted baskets and moccasins. The tents gave way to more permanent structures and soon a cluster of buildings dotted the shoreline. Only a few of those cabins remain today. In one, you will find Frank and Phoebe Roads, still selling their craftwork to visitors.

1J   OAK GABLES/ DISAPPEARING PROPELLER BOAT COMPANY

The patriarch of the boatbuilding fraternity in Port Carling was W.J. Johnston Sr. The townsfolk called him "Uncle Billy Wagtail" because he wore a swallow-tailed coat that jigged like a bird's tail when he walked. Uncle Billy's father was Benjamin Hardcastle Johnston, the founding father of Port Carling. Uncle Billy built his first rowboat around 1869 and eventually had a fleet of rental boats and liveries established in Port Carling, Port Sandfield and Windermere.

Later he built sailboats and launches in partnership with his nephew, Young Billy (W.J. Johnston Jr.), who built the beautiful brick house called Oak Gables in 1924. The Johnstons patented the disappearing propeller device and began building disappearing propeller boats, or "dippies," in a factory behind the house. The Disappearing Propeller Boat Company had a relatively short production run, yet the dippies it produced are among the most prized possessions on the lakes today.

The dippy is a quirky little craft, best described as a glorified wooden rowboat — pointy at both ends, with polished wooden seats and a gasoline engine mounted in the middle. A jointed propeller shaft extended from a metal housing into the water. If the boat hit a log, the propeller "disappeared" into its metal housing like a turtle into its shell.

The end of the First World War signalled a period of prosperity for the

Natives sold baskets and beadwork from cabins built at Indian Village. MUSKOKA LAKES MUSEUM

The old Port Carling school now houses the municipal offices of the Township of Muskoka Lakes.
MUSKOKA LAKES MUSEUM

dippy company, which opened a branch plant in Tonawanda, New York. By 1922 the company was the largest motorboat-building operation in Canada and its success enticed the Bank of Nova Scotia to Port Carling.

Then, just as suddenly as it came on the scene, the Disappearing Propeller Boat Company did a disappearing act of its own. Times had changed. The plant suffered financial difficulties and folded in 1924. It re-opened again, briefly, in 1925.

1K KNOX PRESBYTERIAN CHURCH

Leaving the locks area of Port Carling, you travel up Blacksmith's Hill (so called because of a blacksmith shop once located here) and pass Knox Presbyterian Church, one of the oldest buildings still standing in Port Carling. The church was built in 1876 on a site donated by the Bailey family. Prior to 1876, services were held in the Polar Star Hotel.

LL ST. JAMES ANGLICAN CHURCH

The first Anglican church was built up the street in 1875. When John Fraser erected the Stratton House beside the church, noise from the hotel began to disturb services. The wardens procured the present site from the Roman Catholic church in 1912. (The Roman Catholics had decided not to attempt building a church in the Orangemen's enclave of Port Carling.) Two months later a fire destroyed both the Stratton House and the old Anglican church. This misfortune put pressure on the members of the congregation to get the new church built quickly, which they did within a year.

1M PORT CARLING SCHOOL (Municipal Building)

The location of the Port Carling school skipped about town before settling here in 1906. Since then there have been two additions, the first in 1924, and the second in 1949. There were no electric lights in the school until 1922.

In June, 1960 students of the continuation school were bused to high school in Bracebridge. The school closed in 1969 and is now used as the Muskoka Lakes Township Municipal Office. During renovations in the municipal building in 1975, workers uncovered an entire wall of blackboard space, with the writing still intact. The writing dated to May and June of 1911. According to former clerk-administrator Paul Davidson, the blackboards are still there, behind the new panelling in the planning department.

How Lake Muskoka Got Its Name

Lake Muskoka, the largest of the Muskoka lakes, is named after Ojibway chief Mesqua Ukee (also spelled Musquakie or Misquuckkey in some references). Alexander Shirreff referred to the waters of "Muskoka" in 1829, citing the traders as the originators of the name, after an Indian chief who hunted in the area.

Mesqua Ukee helped the British during the War of 1812, and the conflict left his face scarred. To the Indians his name meant "He who is not easily turned back in battle." The British called him William Yellowhead.

Mesqua Ukee's base of operation was centred at the Narrows, near Orillia, but he claimed all the land in the Muskoka district as his hunting ground. The natives ceded all their land to the British in a series of treaties, but continued to summer in Muskoka following the creation of a reservation at Rama.

Although it is generally agreed that the name Muskoka is derived from a variant form of Mesqua Ukee, other suggestions have been put forward. Surveyor David Thompson spoke of the Muskako Skow See Pie, an Indian term meaning "Swamp Ground River." The derivation of Muskoka in this case would be Swamp Ground.

A well-known Muskoka Indian, Chief Bigwin, once translated the word Muskoka as "red sand," "earth" or "sandy ground." Still another hypothesis is that of Vernon Wadsworth. He believed the district was named after the powerful medicine man, Musquedo, of Indian Village, Port Carling.

2   MUSKOKA LAKES TOWNSHIP PARK

The drive from Port Carling to Bracebridge covers a rolling terrain that often reveals glimpses of sparkling blue bays. Just past Brandy Lake there's a picnic spot on the shores of Lake Muskoka. The beach is sandy, and the water is shallow and clear, perfect for swimming.

Just past the park, you have a choice of taking a sidetrip through the village of Milford Bay, or continuing along Muskoka Road 118 through the famous Huckleberry rock cut. If you don't mind a bit of backtracking, you can do both.

View of Beaumaris wharf, with the Beaumaris Hotel in the background.
PHOTO COURTESY OF IAN TURNBULL

3 SIDETRIP TO MILFORD BAY/BEAUMARIS

(Distance: five kilometres)

Turning right at the Milford Bay Road takes you through the village of Milford Bay and on to Beaumaris.

One of the early settlers in this area was Robert Stroud, who came to Canada in 1873. He cultivated a large farm and orchard here, and supplemented his income as a builder. In 1887 he constructed a stately summer hotel called Milford Bay House at the base of Huckleberry Rock, a popular lookout and blueberry-picking spot. Stroud ran a quiet resort, favoured by clergy. The hotel burned in 1933.

Stroud, a staunch Methodist, was likely turning in his grave when the former hotel site became an infamous "watering hole" called Inn on the Bay. The Township of Muskoka Lakes bought the property in the early 1990s, demolished the building and established a swimming beach and picnic spot called Baycliffe Park. The park officially opened on August 12, 1995. The public lands also extend up the hillside, where the municipality hopes to establish a hiking trail.

Other settlers in the Milford Bay area turned to the resort business in later years. Thomas Mears set up Roseneath Inn on property adjacent the bridge to Tondern Island around 1905. His neighbour, Harry Sawyer built Cedar Wild a few years later. Roseneath is no longer in existence. The Cedar Wild property became Milford Manor, which has since closed. The resort's pitch and putt golf course, which you pass on your way through the village, is still in use.

On leaving Milford Bay, turn right on Beaumaris Road to visit the community of Beaumaris, where many of Muskoka's first well-to-do cottagers built their stately summer homes.

Paul Dane purchased Tondern Island in 1868. Around that time a tiny Danish village called Tondern had captured world attention when it was swallowed up by Germany. Dane called the island Tondern as a symbolic gesture. In 1873 John Willmott and his brother-in-law Edward Prowse purchased the island. Willmott took the north half and Prowse took the south (the road divides their holdings). The name Beaumaris can be traced to the great affection the families had for a vacation spot called Beaumaris on the Isle of Anglesey, Wales.

By this time many sportsmen and vacationers had descended on Muskoka and Edward Prowse saw the wisdom of starting a summer resort. The hotel started in the Prowses, big white house. By 1887 the Beaumaris Hotel had became a fashionable summer retreat, with accommodation for 150 guests. The tourists so enjoyed their time in Muskoka that they purchased properties nearby and built the large summer homes now referred to as "Millionaires Row." Many of the summer residents were bankers or industrialists from the Pittsburgh area, which explains the community's nickname: Little Pittsburgh.

An arsonist set the Beaumaris Hotel afire in July 1945, but John Willmott's original home still survives. It's the pretty white building with green shutters on the corner, opposite St. John Anglican Church.

4   HUCKLEBERRY ROCK CUT

Probably the longest rock cut in Ontario, the Huckleberry rock cut is an impressive sight. The high walls of rose-coloured granite make it look like a long pink tunnel. Very pink, I might add. Its colour is a distinguishing feature.

Although the cut has been blasted, its smooth sections look as if they've been sliced apart like slabs of butter. The road project began in 1962 and caused a flurry of activity among rockhounds, who carted away pieces of the pretty rock for their collections.

5   TAMWOOD LODGE

Built of logs in the old-fashioned style, Tamwood Lodge looks like it might be one of Muskoka's earliest inns. It was actually constructed in 1945 for Dr. Fraser Greig and his wife Jean. They called it Tamarac Lodge when it finally opened in 1948. Builders used local logs, including some tamarack from a nearby property. It is considered to be one of the longest log structures in Canada. The name changed to Tamwood in the late 1960s, when Frank Miller, a former premier of Ontario, owned the property.

In 1967 James Allen founded Muskoka Lakes College at Tamwood after resigning his post as the proposed headmaster at the newly established Rosseau Lake College. A policy rift with the school directors in Rosseau led him to try his hand at a school of his own. Allen's liberal outlook was advanced for the time, and the Tamwood boys' school folded in 1971. For some years the resort was owned operated by Eileen and Fred Reville, in partnership with Miller. Bryan and Marilyn Smith purchased Tamwood in 1982 and built the conference and recreation centre. Anne and Ron Boyd are the current owners.

Follow Muskoka Road 118 into Bracebridge and turn right at the Manitoba Street intersection. The route takes you down the main street of Bracebridge.

6   BRACEBRIDGE

Situated as it is in the centre of the district, Bracebridge seems the logical choice for a town site. But geographic position wasn't the only determining factor. Early surveyors and roadbuilders expected Muskoka Falls to become the destination town in the area. That's where two colonization roads met: the Muskoka Road going north and the Peterson Road going east. Fate and enterprise were in Bracebridge's favour, however.

In 1862 Alexander Bailey built a sawmill at the foot of the falls, followed in 1865 by the first grist mill — for six years the only grist mill in the district. For settlers who had previously travelled to Orillia to get their flour (in some cases walking) the Bracebridge operation was a godsend.

The launching of A. P. Cockburn's steamer *Wenonah* in 1866 sealed the fate of the two communities. The north branch of the Muskoka River provided ready access to Bracebridge. The shallowness of the south branch kept Muskoka Falls out of the navigation loop.

After that it was all over but the rubber stamping, which came in 1868 when the government recognized Bracebridge as the district seat by establishing a district court and Crown Lands office in the community.

The citizens of Bracebridge were never ones to rest on their laurels, however. The first objective was to have the community incorporated as a village — the first in Muskoka. As such, officials instructed John Dobbin to take a count of inhabitants to see if there were indeed enough people living in

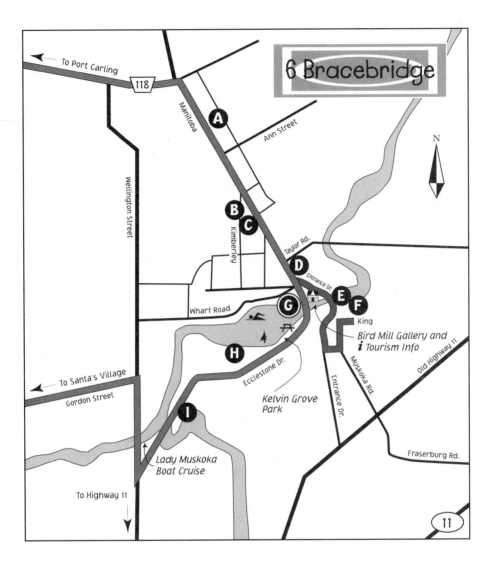

the area. By luck, or good planning, there happened to be an excursion group in Bracebridge the day of the census and Dobbin's report was favourably received. Bracebridge became a village in January 1875.

That very year they began advertising in Toronto newspapers, offering a bonus of $2,000 to manufacturing firms who would establish industries in Bracebridge, as the Bird Woollen Mill had in 1872. Over the years this offer attracted several companies, notably two tanneries: the Beardmore Company in 1877 and Shaw, Cassils and Company in 1891.

Shaw Enterprises came to be known as the Anglo-Canadian Leather Company. Abbott Conway, grandson of C. O. Shaw, once said, "When the

Bracebridge street scene (looking uptown) showing the Bird Mill Bridge and the railway bridge, with the Bird Woollen Mill in-between. The photographer waited for the right moment to catch the steam locomotive heading out of town. ONTARIO ARCHIVES 15963-18

Anglo-Canadian and Beardmore companies were both operating in Bracebridge, it is probable that Bracebridge was the largest centre of heavy leather tanning in the British Empire."

Although large-scale manufacturing still plays a role in the Bracebridge economy, tourism is a dominating feature. The town is in a commanding location, built on rocky slopes above a roaring waterfall. Indeed, the town is blessed with an extraordinary number of impressive waterfalls, which become the focal point during the Festival of the Falls in the spring.

Situated as it is on the 45th parallel of latitude, "halfway between the equator and the North Pole," the community advertises itself as Santa's summer home. Santa's Village attracts thousands of visitors each season, in a community where it's Christmas all year long.

6A JOHN BEAL'S LOCATION

In 1860, when John Beal came to Bracebridge, the colonization road had not yet reached the area. Beal built a log shanty on a site just north of the present Manitoba/Ann Street intersection. It is probable that the location of his shanty set the course of the Muskoka Road (now Manitoba Street) in the Bracebridge area. Historian R.J. Boyer suggests that the roadbuilders elected to run the road past Beal's shanty so he could benefit from the service and help maintain the road.

6B MEMORIAL PARK

In 1900, the Boer War in South Africa was uppermost in the minds of the citizens of Bracebridge. They followed the battles in the newspaper reports, celebrating the victories and mourning the defeats. To honour the memory of the two local volunteers who had died in the battles, the citizens created Memorial Park and sent a request to the Canadian government for two Boer War cannons to be placed on the grounds. (The cannons received were not from the Boer War, however.) Later the town changed the name of the street beside the park to Kimberley Avenue, Kimberley being a town in South Africa.

There is also a plaque outlining details of the early history of Bracebridge and its incorporation as a village in 1875.

6C RENE CAISSE LANE

The street at the end of Memorial Park was renamed Rene Caisse Lane in honour of one of Bracebridge's famous citizens, nurse Rene Caisse. Her herbal remedy for the treatment of cancer received such glowing tributes that patients came to Bracebridge by the busload to see her. The town council helped her establish a clinic in the old British Lion Hotel (now the law office of Lee, Roche and Kelly).

Rene Caisse was born in Bracebridge. Her father owned a barber shop where Owl Pen bookstore is today. When she was training as a nurse in Haileybury, she met a woman who'd been cured of breast cancer with the aid of a Indian remedy made of herbs. She wrote the recipe down and it became the basis of her herbal remedy, Essiac (Caisse spelled backwards).

Although Caisse's treatments helped countless cancer patients, her critics in the medical profession remained skeptical. She faced imprisonment or fines if she dared treat a patient who was not referred by a doctor. The pressure forced the closure of the clinic in 1942. During the 1950s and '60s, Rene Caisse lived in the pretty brick house at the corner of Rene Caisse Lane and Kimberley Avenue (Ronald Burk Law Office).

6D OLD POST OFFICE AND CUSTOM BUILDING

Postal service began in 1864 in the store run by pioneer settler Alexander Bailey (see 6G below). When the settlers applied for a post office their community was known as North Falls. The name Bracebridge comes from a book by Washington Irving entitled *Bracebridge Hall*, which a secretary in the Post Office Department happened to be reading at the time.

In the 1890s Mr. Perry ran the post office in a building where the Pelican Bay store is today. Construction on the Taylor and Manitoba Street post office was under way in 1914. The limestone corner blocks and window sills came labelled and ready to put in place, all the way from Scotland. The tower supports the town clock, which chimes every hour.

The import-export business of the tanneries and the woollen mill prompted the need for a customs office, which opened in this building in 1911.

6E BIRD MILL BRIDGE

The Bird Mill bridge marks the location of the original bridge into Bracebridge. From here the road to Muskoka Falls led up a steep hill — now open only to agile pedestrians. At the top of the hill, however, the old road still exists (for a short distance) and is called Muskoka Road South.

When the first settlers came here, the only way to cross the falls was on a pine log. James Cooper is said to have felled the tree they crossed on. Other early settlers were John Beal, David Leith and Hiram McDonald. Leith built on land where the town hall is now located and McDonald owned a rough log tavern called, of all things, the Royal Hotel. A story tells how a drunken settler, on his way home from the Royal, slipped off the log bridge and was saved when the strap on his drinking flask caught on the stub of a branch. This fortunate man could claim that liquor had been his salvation.

The first bridge (built when the colonization road went through in 1861) has been replaced several times, most recently in 1991.

6F WOODCHESTER VILLA/CHAPEL GALLERY

If I could live in any restored home I wished, I'd choose Woodchester Villa. When you visit the place you understand why. Built in 1882 by manufacturing magnate Henry Bird, the building is the dream home of any reader of romance novels. All the features are there: stained glass, enclosed porch, wrap-around balcony, a rose arbor. The unique octagonal structure graces the plateau of a wooded hillside above the town. The kitchen is on the lowest level. Judging from the narrowness of the passage leading from there to the "master's" domain, the servants risked getting stuck if they gained a few pounds. From the kitchen level a dumbwaiter runs up the centre of the house. This allowed the Bird sisters to take tea on the rooftop lookout without the bother of carrying the tray up the stairs.

The theories of Mr. Orson Fowler influenced Bird's house design. Its octagonal shape reflected the builder's desire to conform to more spherical forms found in nature. No doubt Bird's neighbours thought it strange, but Bird had a lighthearted response to their queries. "I'm building a bird cage to keep my Birds in," he'd say.

The Bracebridge Rotary Club restored the Bird home and the site is operated by the Bracebridge Historical Society.

Henry Bird's octagonal home, Woodchester Villa, had a dumbwaiter running up the centre of the building, and a rooftop lookout where the Bird sisters sometimes had their afternoon tea.
PHOTO COURTESY OF PETER WOOD

The Chapel Gallery adjoins Woodchester Villa. Operated by Muskoka Arts and Crafts since the fall of 1989, the gallery is housed in a replica of the first Presbyterian church in Bracebridge, built in this location. The gallery sponsors exhibits of work by members and other provincial artists. It also hosts workshops in the arts. The Muskoka School of the Arts operates from the gallery during the summer months.

6G BRACEBRIDGE BAY PARK

There are two parking areas that give access to Bracebridge Bay: on the west side of the river off Wharf Road and on the east side at Kelvin Grove Park.

Now it's time for confessions. Before researching this book, I didn't realize that one of the best historic spots in Muskoka was in the town where I spent much of the working day. I've always admired the falls as I've whizzed by to do the shopping. I've even picnicked by the water, and crossed the walkway to feel the roar and mist of the torrent. But I'd never taken the time to walk around the entire bay and read the historic markers. These aren't regular historic markers, either. The Town (much to its credit) has pictures at each site showing what you'd have seen years ago.

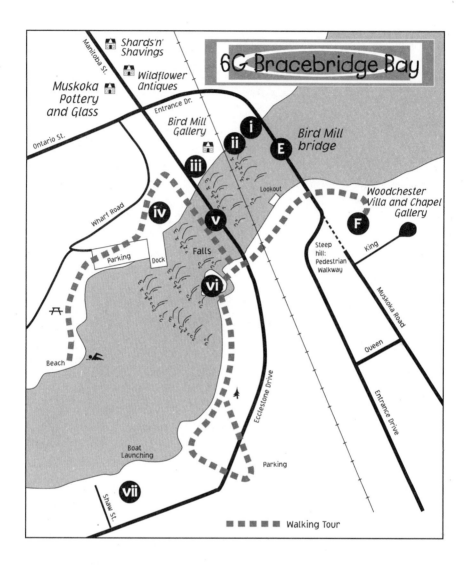

i) First Generating Plant

Mr. W.S. Shaw built the first hydro-electric generating station in a small building at the top of the falls. It supplied the electricity for Shaw's tannery farther down the river and for the streetlights in the town. In 1894 the Town of Bracebridge bought the generating station and, in doing so, became the first Ontario municipality to own its own power plant. Later, when the town built a bigger facility at the bottom of the falls, the plant became a water-pumping station. Although the pumps are now run by electricity, the original water-powered turbines are on site for emergency use.

ii) The Bird Woollen Mill

Bracebridge had not yet achieved village status when Mr. Henry Bird arrived on the scene in 1872 and established the Bird Woollen Mill. The mill foundations are visible on the west side of the river between the Bird Mill bridge and the railway bridge. The original mill looked rather pretty in this spot. It was a three-and-a-half-storey wooden building that served as a family residence as well as a mill until the Birds moved into Woodchester Villa.

Bird had been looking for a location that had water power and suitable grazing land for sheep. He found them both in Muskoka. Bird helped farmers establish their flocks of sheep, ensuring a good supply of raw wool. Eventually he imported wool from Australia when the local flocks declined.

Over the years the little wooden mill became enclosed in stone and concrete additions that came within a hair's breath of the town's first generating station. The mill made Mackinaw jackets, which were popular with lumbermen because of their water resistance. They also made a variety of thick wool blankets, including the Indian Point blankets developed for the tourist market. The end of the logging boom meant less demand for mackinaw jackets. That fact, coupled with the introduction of synthetic fibres, forced the mill to close in 1954. The Town of Bracebridge has since demolished the buildings and smoothed the rubble into a parking lot.

iii) Bird Mill Mews

For years the last surviving building of the Bird Woollen Mill stood grey and desolate between the railway and the Silver Bridge. Today it's a focal point in the town, housing the Chamber of Commerce office, an art gallery and restaurant. The Town of Bracebridge purchased the warehouse and began renovating it in 1993. The unique stone countertop in the chamber office came from the chapel of the Society of St. John the Evangelist in Bracebridge. Look closely in the corners and centre of the stone and you'll see small carved crosses from the days when it was the altar in the church.

iv) Second Generating Plant

It looks more like a country cottage than a generating station. The stone walls and dormer windows make this the most attractive hydro-electric station in Canada. What's more, it's the oldest one still in operation. The project began in 1900. By placing the generator at the foot of the falls, the plant could take advantage of the entire drop of water and so produce more energy. The plant has been in continuous operation since 1902. If you'd like to look inside, just knock on the door and a staff member will be happy to show you around.

v) Silver Bridge

Prior to 1930 there was no road connection on the south side of the railway tracks. Surveys for the new roadway (Ecclestone Drive) were underway in 1928. The bridge was built in 1935.

vi) Grist Mill

A little water wheel marks the site of Alexander Bailey's grist mill on the rocks to the east side of the falls. When Bailey completed the mill in 1865, he had a rather stark utilitarian structure, three and a half storeys high. Water entered the mill turbine via a diversion weir at the edge of the falls. You can still see the remains of the weir there today. In 1869 Bailey sold his mill to Thomas Myers and Robert Perry and moved to Port Carling. Perry and Myers converted the stone milling process to a roller mill and ran a thriving business — up to 75 barrels of flour per day. The grist mill burned in 1909.

vii) Minett-Shields Boatworks

Landscaped grounds and a park setting make pleasant surroundings for the people living in the townhouses beside the park. In 1923, however, this was the site of the famous Minett-Shields Boatworks. The founder of the company, Bert Minett, began building launches at the family resort, Clevelands House. In 1910 he moved to Bracebridge and set up shop in the ground floor of the chair factory (Hess Furniture Company, now Northern Buildall). A partnership with Bryson Shields in 1925 helped save the business at a critical period.

The company built its reputation on perfection. Not a boat left the shop unless it satisfied Minett's criterion that nothing else could be done to improve it. During the war years Minett-Shields, in conjunction with the Port Carling Boatworks, built 50-foot harbour craft used in World War Two. These boats often made trial runs down the Muskoka River. With the advent of fibreglass hulls, the boatworks closed in 1948.

6H ANGLO-CANADIAN LEATHER COMPANY

In 1891 W. Sutherland Shaw came to Bracebridge to manage the Shaw, Cassils tannery, later known as the Anglo-Canadian Leather Company. The leather company also operated a plant in Huntsville, which was managed by C.O. Shaw. Local people often referred to the Shaw enterprise as the "new" tannery, the first being the Beardmore Tanning Company located farther downriver.

The Anglo-Canadian Leather Company's Bracebridge operation closed in 1930 when the Americans placed a tariff on sole leather. At that time the

Anglo-Canadian company sold most of its product to American markets. The Huntsville branch of the company remained open until 1960.

The tanneries found a plentiful supply of tanbark in Muskoka's hemlock trees —previously considered "trash" by the lumbermen. The companies produced leather by treating the hides with tannic acid found in the bark of hemlock. The heavy leather produced by Anglo-Canadian found its best market in providing the soles for logging boots, which were designed to have corks driven into them. The Anglo-Canadian leather had the ability to cling to the corks and hold fast when a man's weight hit a log. Anglo-Canadian leather was unique in this way, and the only such leather produced in the world.

The tannery site is now a condominium development called River Edge Estates.

6-I J.D. SHIER LUMBER AND SUPPLY MILLS

Brightly coloured flags flap above the cars on this dealer's lot, but at the turn of the century you would have seen piles of sawdust and lumber. In the early 1880s J.D. Shier and Singleton Brown ran the sawmill in this location. The partnership dissolved soon after it began, and Shier ran the mill on his own. His supply of logs came from the Lake of Bays area, driven down the south branch of the Muskoka River and clearing waterfalls with the aid of log slides. In 1898 the mill burned. Shier rebuilt on a larger scale and with better equipment. His double-cutting band mill was the first in Canada. At one time a railway siding ran to both the Anglo-Canadian Leather Company and Shier's sawmill to provide access to the main line.

7   SIDE TRIP TO SANTA'S VILLAGE

(Distance: 4.8 kilometres)

Continue to the intersection of Ecclestone Drive and Wellington Street (Muskoka Road 118). Turn right across the bridge. Turn left on Santa's Village Road .

Billed as "The Summer Home of the Christmas Spirit," Santa's Village is a popular attraction, especially for families with small and not-so-small children. Along with the amusement-park rides there are wonderland adventures on the Kris Kringle paddlewheel boat cruise and the Candy Cane Express. There's more than enough to see and do — including go-cart rides, mini-golf, mountain bike riding, batting cages, laser tag, rollerblading trails and an arcade. It will take two or three visits to experience everything.

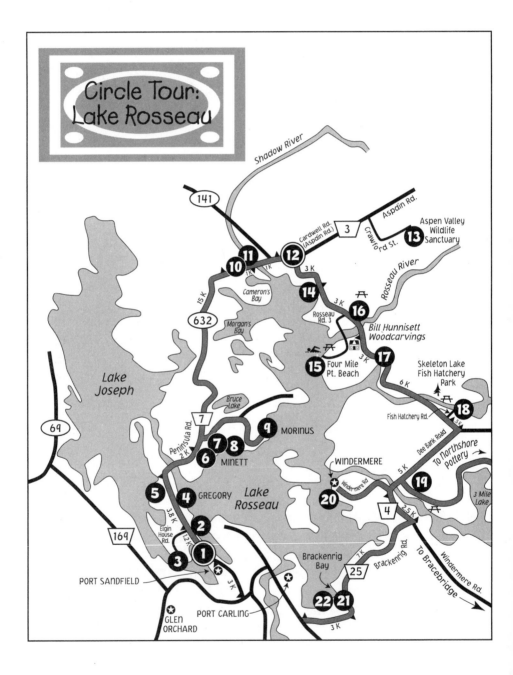

Circle Tour: Lake Rosseau

CHAPTER 4

Circle Tour of Lake Rosseau

Distance: 57 kilometres (35 miles), not including side trips

"There is one thing which Muskoka possesses in a pre-eminent degree
and that is its wonderful health-restoring climate ... The sun does not
reach the meridian until some time later than it does in Toronto,
and the rocky nature of the country seems to retain the heat
until late in the evening, making it comfortable and pleasant to sit
outdoors without any extra clothing until an hour when it would be
not only uncomfortable, but really dangerous to do so in Toronto."

from Beatrice Scovell's *The Muskoka Story*

If any part of Muskoka looks as if it could restore your strength, the land around Lake Rosseau does. Toronto physicians often encouraged their patients to summer in Muskoka. In most cases those who came here to recover their health did. Even now the land seems pristine. Certainly there are more cottages than in earlier days and more fast boats on the lake, but there are also long stretches of shoreline and roadway with nothing to see but deliciously cool Muskoka bush.

Along this route, you'll see the fabled Windermere House, which rose again from the ashes after a devastating fire in 1996. You will get glimpses of Lake Joseph, the lake the Indians called "The Clear Water."

The name Rosseau can be traced to fur trader Jean Baptiste Rousseau, who travelled throughout this area in the late 1820s. Rousseau named lakes Rosseau and Joseph after his father, Joseph Rousseau. Over the years the first "u" has been dropped in Rosseau.

Starting in Port Sandfield, the tour travels up the west side of the lake, along Peninsula Road, to Rosseau, then down the east shoreline to the dramatic cliffs of Skeleton Bay. From here the route travels inland, then returns to the lake via Dee Bank falls, Windermere and Brackenrig Bay, joining Muskoka Road 118 just south of Port Carling.

— SIGHTS —

Port Sandfield Canal
St. George's Church
Christ Church Gregory
St. John the Baptist Church,
   Morinus
Victoria Rock
Nipissing Colonization Road
Shadow River

Aspen Valley Wildlife Sanctuary
Four Mile Point Beach
Rosseau River Rapids
Skeleton Lake
   Fish Hatchery Park
Dee Bank Falls
Windermere House
Penney's Sawmill

— ARTS AND CRAFTS —

The Craft Room
Highway 141
Rosseau
705-732-6206

Bill Hunnisett Woodcarvings
Off Highway 141 at Fry Road
705-732-6323
By appointment

Northshore Pottery
Off Northshore Road
(turn right at Sandwood Road)
705-769-2352

— ANTIQUES —

Rosseau Lake Antiques
Highway 141
Rosseau

1   PORT SANDFIELD

There's a certain charm to the village of Port Sandfield that tempts you to stop and spend some time. The village has a timeless appeal. You can enter the door of a pioneer church and admire the craftsmanship of the early settlers, and wonder about its tiny cemetery, where a brave stone cross defies the elements of time. Strolling along a classic wooden boardwalk, you'll find an old freight shed that's been lovingly restored. It dates back to the days when steamboats passed through the canal like clockwork.

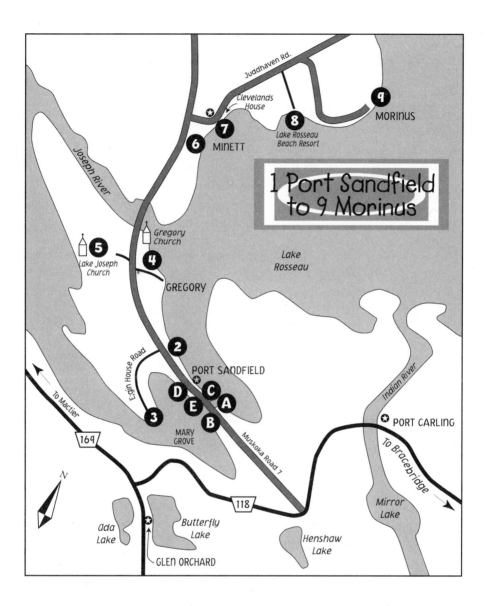

IA THE CANAL

At one time a narrow spit of sand was all that separated Lake Rosseau and Lake Joseph. To the north, the Joe River provided access between the two lakes, but it was full of rocks and difficult to navigate. Settlers preferred to portage across the sand. One enterprising family, the Foremans, rented out their team of horses to haul boats from one lake to the other.

In 1870, in the interests of improving navigation, the Public Works department started dredging a canal. Work on the canal was under way in

Prospect House, at Port Sandfield on regatta day. MUSKOKA LAKES MUSEUM

1870 when a government delegation travelled this way. In the entourage were John Carling, Commissioner of Public Works, and Premier John Sandfield Macdonald. The men camped out on the lakeshore. Before setting out the next day they took time to name the spot in honour of the premier. The words Port Sandfield were carved into a pine plank and nailed to a tree.

When the canal opened in the autumn of 1871, the steamer *Wenonah* got stuck during the official ceremonies and the Public Works department had to bring the dredging machine back for another round. The canal opened the following year.

Today the canal is shaded by a canopy of deciduous trees that casts leafy patterns on the boardwalk. You can meander from one side to the other and gaze at both lakes, or laze on the banks and watch the boats go by.

The first wooden bridge looked like it was erected on stilts. The height allowed steamboats to pass underneath, but discouraged pedestrians.

The old swing bridge at Port Sandfield. PHOTO BY G.W.CAMPBELL

1B THE BRIDGE

In 1876 construction crews put up a tall wooden bridge that was great for the steamboats, but not much fun for pedestrians. They had to huff and puff their way up the steep inclines, then pluck up their courage to cross to the other side. The bridge developed such a terrible sway that people were afraid to walk on it. A new wooden swing bridge was installed in 1887, which was followed by a metal swing bridge in 1924. That bridge survived until just recently and was the last hand-swung bridge in Ontario. It opened for the final time on September 6, 1997, when the *Wanda III* passed underneath. For safety reasons, it was replaced with a hydraulic bridge in 1998.

1C PROSPECT HOUSE

For many years the only landmark in Port Sandfield was the stilt-like wooden bridge that crossed the canal. Then Enoch Cox appeared on the scene and built a 25-guest boarding house in 1881. Later he expanded the business, erecting the stately Prospect House. By 1888 the hotel had grown to accommodate 300 people. It stood on the north side of the bridge, a splendid edifice by the standards of the day. It boasted a ballroom, music room and other features of refinement. The Cox family had been introduced to Muskoka by John Rogers, a cartographer who mapped all the Muskoka Lakes.

Prospect House burned on October 15, 1916.

St. George's church. Built in 1883, the church still opens its doors for an annual church service each summer. PHOTO BY SUSAN PRYKE

1D ST. GEORGE'S CHURCH

One of the picturesque spots in the village is St. George's church, which survives today due to the dedication of the local residents. Built in 1883, the pioneer church is open to the public every day during the summer. Once a year, on the Civic Holiday weekend, a memorial service is held.

Enoch and Sarah Cox donated the land for the church. Buried next to the church is George Edward Cox and his wife Christina, proprietors of Prospect House when it burned.

1E MICKLETHWAITE'S PHOTOGRAPHY SHOP

Muskoka's photographic chronicler, Frank Micklethwaite, once washed glass negatives at the Prospect House swimming beach (where Port Sandfield Marina is located today). He struck a deal with Enoch Cox to take pictures of guests and events at the hotel. From a humble studio on the shore of Lake Joseph, Micklethwaite developed thousands of pictures of Muskoka from 1892 to 1910.

W.J. JOHNSTON BOAT LIVERY

The Port Sandfield Marina was originally W.J. Johnston's boat livery. The disappearing propeller boat was invented here in 1914 by Billy Johnston Jr., with help from Edwin Rogers.

2   JOHN ROGERS' HOME (Birchwood)

We remember Capt. John Rogers as the cartographer who drew all the maps for the *Guide Book and Atlas of Muskoka and Parry Sound Districts*. But before he came to Port Sandfield, he was a man of the world. He worked on the railway, studied law, built diving machines and worked in Arabia on a project to distill seawater. A chance meeting with a couple aboard ship in 1871, convinced Rogers to come to Muskoka. He had no money to speak of, just a willingness to try new things. He helped clear land for settlers when he arrived in Port Sandfield.

Seymour Penson, who did the sketches for the 1879 atlas, said Rogers had a fund of knowledge on every subject. "Certain places seem to fit certain natures, and Muskoka certainly suited John Rogers," Penson said of his friend. "The freedom from restraint; the ever-changing climate, with just enough harshness to be piquant; the natural beauty of the place and the abundance of material for scientific experimenting…all these things and many others must have appealed strongly to a man like John Rogers, and they threw over him a spell that has never been broken."

Rogers married Edith May Cox. His second home on this site, Birchwood, is the lovely yellow house with the brown trim near the Elgin House Road turnoff.

3   LAKE JOSEPH CLUB/ELGIN HOUSE

The expansive grounds of the Lake Joseph Club resort are situated on the site of the former Elgin House, one of Muskoka's grand hotels. A blacksmith by trade, Lambert Love moved here from Gravenhurst in 1885. He ran a sawmill where the Lake Joseph Club swimming beach is today. The Loves, like other settlers, took in a few boarders and summer visitors. A trip to the Chicago World's Fair in 1893 impressed Love. He realized what a success the tourism business could be if properly done. In particular he carried back a memory of immaculate grounds, a characteristic that would become the hallmark of Elgin House. As the popularity of the Loves' accommodations grew, their home was soon bulging at the seams. They decided to build a proper hotel, which opened its doors in 1900. The resort grew larger each year and its trim lawns and gardens won it a reputation as a fine resort.

Lambert Love held strict religious views. No drinking or smoking was allowed by either guests or staff. Nor could you wear a bathing suit on Sundays. In spite of these restrictions, the resort was one of the most popular of its era.

Management of the resort passed to Lambert's son Bert, and then Bert's son Victor. In 1969 Victor sold the resort to the Grisé family. The business fell on

Lambert Love's Elgin House.
PHOTO COURTESY OF IAN TURNBULL

difficult times in 1991. The resort remained closed for several years, during which time the old buildings deteriorated. ClubLink Corporations bought the resort and began building the golf course in 1995. By 1997, the first phase of the exclusive accommodation units were ready for vacationers.

The Elgin House chapel is the only building still standing from Lambert Love's era.

4   GREGORY

The community of Gregory received its name in 1880 when William Gregory applied for postal service. He bought land in the area and his son, Richard, opened a summer resort on the Joseph River called Golpha House. The Gregorys came into an inheritance and became known as the Gregory-Allens.

When the family moved out west around 1915, Richard sold the hotel to Mrs. L.T. McKinley, who called it the Nepahwin-Gregory, intriguingly advertised as a summer and winter resort in 1918. It was the first resort to have electric light from its own generating plant.

Today there are only cottages and homes in the area, and a trim pioneer church and cemetery, further up the road, on the Joseph River. Christ Church dates to 1890. It was built on land donated to the Anglican Church by Michael Doyle.

5   LAKE JOSEPH CHURCH

You couldn't find a more serene spot for a church than this pine-clad shore. The sound of the water gently lapping along the rocks loosens all the knots in your back. From here you can see why the Indians called Lake Joseph "The Clear Water." The water is wonderfully transparent.

This was a boat-access church until 1967, when the congregation chipped in to build a road and parking area. The church itself dates back to 1902 when the Mackenzie brothers from Foot's Bay started building it on land purchased by the Presbyterian congregation. The first service was held on August 9, 1903. In 1925, following the union of some Presbyterian and Methodist churches, the Lake Joseph Church became a non-denominational church under the jurisdiction of the United Church.

6   OLD SCHOOLHOUSE

The early settlers organized a school section in this area in 1894 and erected a frame school — called the Gregory School — near the Joseph River bridge. In 1932 they built a brick school near the Minett corner. Children took their lessons here until 1958.

SIDE TRIP TO MORINUS
(Distance: 5.7 kilometres)
At Minett Corners, turn east on the Juddhaven Road (Muskoka Road 28). Be alert for deer browsing on the roadsides during the autumn.

7   MINETT AND CLEVELANDS HOUSE

The community of Minett takes its name from the first pioneers in the area. Charles James Minett came to Canada to improve his opportunity for success. He was the sixth son of a large family and saw no chance of rising further than a tradesman if he stayed in England. After working two years as a carpenter in Toronto, Minett took up free grant land here in Medora Township in 1869.

The Minett family cleared the land for farming and later took tourists into their home — called Cleeve Lands, after Bishop Cleeve, the village where Charles was born. The establishment grew into a prosperous summer resort. The printers dropped an "e" when they printed the hotel's first register, and it has been spelled Clevelands House since then. The hotel, at one time, had lawn bowling greens and private stables, as well as productive gardens and pastures. All the hotel's vegetables, milk, butter, eggs and meat were produced on the farm.

Guests arrived by steamer in the early days, which gave Charles the idea of making his hotel look like a ship. When it came time for him to add a third storey, he incorporated a mansard roof and octagonal tower, which resembled the pilothouse of a very large lake steamer.

During the construction of this addition, in 1891, Charles fell and received injuries that eventually led to his death. The second generation Minetts built the North Lodge, or annex, in the spot where the family's first log home had been.

Bob Cornell, the present owner, once worked as a bellhop at Clevelands House, then as manager. He purchased the resort in 1969. Clevelands House today is a pleasing mix of the modern and the traditional. The main lodge retains its wrap-around verandah and Old Muskoka look, while the new reception area gleams with marble and brass. Tidy walkways zigzag from building to building, each flanked with cascades of flowers and shrubbery.

8   LAKE ROSSEAU BEACH RESORT/ PAIGNTON HOUSE

The Lake Rosseau Beach Resort property was the homestead of J. Frederick Pain, a rather well-to-do Englishmen, who was born in Calcutta. When his doctor advised him to move to a colder climate to ward off his bouts of malaria, Pain thought of his acquaintances, the Wrenshalls and the Besleys, who had taken up land on the shores of Lake Rosseau. He moved to this spot in the 1870s after trying out some other locations. Fred named the resort Paignton House after his birthplace, Paignton, England. The Pains ran the resort until the 1970s, when the Granite Group took over. Today it is owned by Ken Fowler, who plans to turn the resort into a major conference centre with a championship golf course.

Continue along the Juddhaven Road to the Morinus turnoff.

9   ST. JOHN THE BAPTIST CHURCH (1233 Juddhaven Road)

I couldn't think of a better place to put a church than a rocky promontory overlooking Lake Rosseau. There's a humble greatness to this little building — so white and clean with its twin spires projecting into the bright blue sky.

William McNaughton gave the land to the local Roman Catholic mission in 1899. In the next two years the local residents raised money and built the church, which was blessed by Bishop O'Connor on July 22, 1902.

Many people come by boat to celebrate mass here on Sunday mornings. If you walk (carefully) down to the wharf and look to your right, you'll see the rocky outcrop called Victoria Rock. When viewed from a certain angle, it resembles the profile of Queen Victoria.

Summer chairs at Clevelands House.
PHOTO BY G.W. CAMPBELL

Return to Minett Corners and continue travelling north on Peninsula Road. Hold on to your hat! The road gets twisty, but it's worth it! The same road eventually becomes Parry Sound District Road 632 — a real roller-coaster ride.

10 CAMERON BAY - Starting Point for the Nipissing Colonization Road

The road takes a sharp turn around the foot of Cameron's Bay, where a large grey residence looks out at the bay. The Nipissing Colonization Road, seen behind the gate on the left as you turn the corner, ran 107 kilometres (67 miles) from this bay north to Nipissing. The pre-confederation government authorized the road in an effort to encourage settlement in the northern districts. Work began on the road in 1866. Before the locks were installed at the Indian River, northbound settlers transferred from a steamboat at Port Carling to a longboat and rowed up to Cameron Bay. Later, when Rosseau became a steamboat port, the settlers disembarked there. They stayed in an immigration shed overnight, then climbed into ox carts to travel up the Nipissing Road.

The Nipissing Road lost its importance after the railway was built from Gravenhurst to Callander in 1886. The stretch from Ashdown Corners to the Bear Cave turnoff is still used by cars and trucks today. Snowmobilers keep the old colonization road brushed out all the way to Seguin Falls Road. A plaque marking the road's starting point has been mounted in the rock near the boathouse at the foot of the bay.

Shadow River. The water's reflective qualities made it a natural curiosity in the early days.

11 SHADOW RIVER

Tourism brochures promoted the Shadow River as a wonderful natural curiosity, whose waters magically reflected the images of overhanging branches. The river received its name because of these reflections, but was earlier called White Oak Creek.

It was here that poet Pauline Johnson took the famous canoe ride that inspired her poem "Shadow River." Johnson was the daughter of a Mohawk chief and an Englishwoman. She and her school friends spent some idyllic summers camping in Muskoka, and Johnson wrote several poems about the area.

12 ROSSEAU

Rosseau was once known as "The Gateway to the West," for it was here that the immigrants embarked on the Nipissing Road for destinations in Northern Ontario and the Prairies. The government provided a hostel for the travellers at the Rosseau shoreline. The so-called "Immigrant Shed" was an inelegant four-room structure designed to house those too poor to afford hotel accommodation.

Until 1870 Rosseau was virtually non-existent. Around 1863 Edward Clifford and a trapper called British Bill owned most of what is now the village of Rosseau. Then came Ebenezer Sirett, "the Squire," who sliced himself a huge

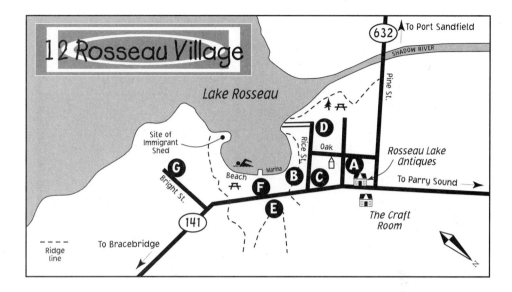

12 Rosseau Village

section of free grant land near Ashdown Corners. The Beley family, who have a point named after them, followed Sirett. At that time community life centred on Ashdown Corners, several kilometres to the north, where there was a store, hotel, post office, church and several homesteads.

The situation changed when W.H. Pratt decided to build a major resort at the north end of Lake Rosseau. Pratt pioneered the wilderness retreat idea, firmly believing that guests would travel to the most inaccessible places if they were treated like royalty once they got there. Just as Pratt had anticipated, people flocked to Rosseau House, which was declared the best hotel in Ontario at that time.

The flurry of activity around the hotel shifted attention away from Ashdown Corners to the lakeside settlement, which was first called Helmsley. Pratt disliked that name, and he also disliked having to travel several miles to Ashdown Corners to pick up his mail, especially as the steamers that brought the mail tied up at his wharf. He passed around a petition asking that a new post office be opened and that its name be Rosseau House.

When the hotel burned in 1883, the post office moved to William Ditchburn's house. The post office stamp, with the word "house" filed off, continued in use in the new location. They say this postal stamp was partly to blame for the village being called Rosseau, even though it was officially Helmsley on land deeds until 1926. Rosseau was incorporated as a village that year.

Ox cart in front of the Rosseau General Store, the oldest building in Rosseau.
PHOTO COURTESY OF PETER WOOD

12A NIPISSING ROAD (Historic Marker)
AND ROSSEAU COMMUNITY HALL

Although the Nipissing Road did not pass through the village of Rosseau, the townspeople decided to place the historic marker here at the community hall, where more people were apt to notice it. The marker details the significance of the early colonization road (see 10 above).

The hall itself is built of native rock in memory of Rosseau's veterans.

12B THE ROSSEAU GENERAL STORE

The Rosseau General Store is a landmark in the village and has been so for about 124 years. It is generally accepted that the store was built in 1874. Certainly the Peacocks were keeping shop here in 1875, as early records show. The exterior of the building has never changed. Inside, the original wood floors ripple with age. The stairs resemble wave-washed rocks, worn wafer thin at their centres. It still has the look of an old-fashioned country store; a place where you can get just about anything you need while on vacation.

12C ROCKY TOP TRADING POST

Rocky Top Trading Post is a perfect companion for the General Store. You'd think the two buildings were part of the same operation. The original store was built in the same era as its partner across the street, but it burned down in 1925.

The owner, George Atkinson, rebuilt on the same site. The new store was almost an exact duplicate of the old one, but without a front verandah.

Atkinson was a colourful character and had his fingers in several pies here in Rosseau. He ran the stage service that met the trains, but also operated a freight office and funeral parlour in this store. The coffins were stacked up on shelves behind the freight. The embalming process took place in another room. Atkinson owned the building from 1922 to 1945, the year he died. The Whytes took over then and did extensive renovation before opening a tea room called "Hilltop."

12D SITE OF PRATT'S ROSSEAU HOUSE

Keep going straight when you drive down Rice Street (it becomes more of a lane than a street). The house on the right at the end of the street marks the site of Rosseau House, which burned in 1883. When W.H. Pratt officially opened the three-storey hotel in 1871 (he built it in 1870 and took a few guests that summer), it looked like a seaside castle, dramatically perched on the headland. At the base of the building, the grounds fell steeply to the lake below. An impressive sight.

Mr. Pratt was a jovial and good-natured host who was well liked about the village. His spirited personality is evident in a comment he made to his friend William Ditchburn as they surveyed the ruins of the hotel after the fire. "Well Ditchburn," he said, "it was a good fire while it lasted. I'm sorry that sawhorse of yours was burned; it should have been returned."

The Rosseau waterfront showing the Monteith House and Ditchburn boat rentals.
PHOTO COURTESY OF PETER WOOD

The lane to the left of the hotel site gives access to the Rosseau park, originally called "Pratt's Grove." The park crowns the top of a high ridge, where short trails take you to numerous rocky ledges where you can look out at the bay.

12E SITE OF MONTEITH HOUSE

From the General Store, the main road (Highway 141) dips down to Lake Rosseau before climbing another hill. There's nothing much in "the dip" now, but in earlier years this was the heart of the village. The pulse-maker here was a large hotel called Monteith House.

John Monteith purchased a small building called the Portland House in 1878 and proceeded to build a large three-storey addition. Later he built a dance hall across the street, now the site of Muskoka Lake Marine, and another three-storey addition.

After John Monteith died, his sons, Arthur and Bert, built up the hotel business and employed a famous singer, John Strathdee, to entertain guests. Strathdee wrote the words and music to "Rosseau Town" and "Rosseau Town Goodbye." In later years the hotel passed into the ownership of the Shopsowitz family of Shopsy's Meats fame. The hotel burned in November 1950.

12F MONTEITH BUTCHER SHOP (Catholic Church)

John Monteith, proprietor of Monteith House, was also a wholesale and retail butcher. It is thought that he helped establish the popularity of Muskoka lamb — at one time a must on the menus of superior establishments. After Monteith's death, the butcher shop near the hotel was renovated as staff lodgings. After the hotel burned, the building became the Catholic Church.

12G EATON SUMMER ESTATE (Rosseau Lake College)

The Ditchburn brothers (William, Henry, John and Arthur) arrived in Helmsley fresh from London, England, in 1869. By 1870 they'd purchased the land that was later known as the Eaton summer estate. The Ditchburns found they were suited to neither farming nor fishing. Fortunately Mr. Pratt had arrived in the area, and he encouraged them to build boats for his guests at Rosseau House.

After the hotel fire the brothers pursued their own interests. Henry began a boatbuilding and rental business, which grew to such proportions that he moved his base of operations to Gravenhurst. In 1906 he sold his property to John and Flora Eaton (later Sir John and Lady Eaton), who built a summer estate called Kawandag, an Ojibway word meaning "the meeting place of the pines."

Kawandag.
The summer home of
Sir John and Lady Eaton.

The trees that inspired the name are much in evidence on this point, but you can't help but wish the mansion-like summer home of Sir John and Lady Eaton were still here.

The estate was a truly grand one: Scottish stonemasons built the foundations and fireplaces, craftsmen from Europe installed the interior woodwork. There was a room to watch the sun rise in, and one to watch the sun set. There were stables, of course, as the Eaton boys loved their horses and often rode up from the family farm at King City in the company of the stable hand. Lady Eaton also had a pretty log cabin, her retreat, which is still standing on the college grounds.

After Sir John's death in 1922, Lady Eaton came to Kawandag less often and eventually decided to sell. The estate was run as an exclusive resort for some years. In the 1960s Roger Morris and Maurice East transformed the grounds into a frontier outpost called Fort Kawandag. Each day they staged a mock battle between Indians and Redcoats and ran stagecoach rides around the property. The fort failed after only two seasons and the estate became a private school, Rosseau Lake College.

The idea to create a private school at the Kawandag site took shape in 1966 and the school was founded in 1967. Rosseau Lake College now offers students an alternative to conventional classroom study through a challenging program that incorporates an outdoor emphasis. During the summer months, Camp Oochigeas operates here, providing a summer camp experience for young cancer patients.

In 1973 a fire demolished the former Eaton mansion, which housed the school library and lounge.

13   ASPEN VALLEY WILDLIFE SANCTUARY
Distance: Five kilometres
(follow Cardwell Road east to Crawford Street)

Twenty-six years ago, a conservation officer asked Audrey Tournay if she would look after an injured raccoon. Since then, hundreds of raccoons have found a temporary home at the Aspen Valley Wildlife Sanctuary, along with countless foxes, deer, porcupines, skunks, beavers, wolves, coyotes, bears, moose, and birds of all description.

While most of the animals will find their way back to the forests and streams of Muskoka, some have become permanent residents. The Michigan bears, for instance, arrived in near-starved condition with no fur and few teeth after being used to train hunting dogs. Today they are plump and sleek, thanks to the sanctuary's expert care, but they will live here the rest of their days. In an effort to make their home as comfortable as possible, Tony Grant, manager of the sanctuary, has built a large enclosure that encompasses a pond and woodland.

Due to incredible interest in the operation, the sanctuary is open to the public on Wednesday and Sunday afternoons during the summer season. At that time you may see some of the animals. The sanctuary relies entirely on donations, so please be sure to make yours before you leave!

14   MUSKOKA WOODS SPORTS RESORT/LAWRASONS

Muskoka Woods is known throughout the world for its excellent sports facilities. Operated by the John Boddy Youth Foundation, the camp provides a Christian focus as well as athletic training. Just about every sport imaginable is taught here, including rollerblading, skiing, sailing, mountain biking, archery, tennis and golf. Gymnastics teams have used Muskoka Woods to train for the Olympics.

The camp is situated on land originally settled by William Lawrason. His wife Julia called her home "The Beach" after the fine stretch of sand along the shore. Her log home was later enlarged as a summer home for Arthur McCrae, Lady Eaton's brother. It is now called The Manor House and is still in use at Muskoka Woods.

15   FOUR MILE POINT BEACH
Distance 1.5 kilometres (Off Highway 141 on Rosseau Road 3)

If the weather's scorching, and you'd like a refreshing dip, turn off Highway 141 at Rosseau Road 3. Follow the road over the Rosseau River to Four Mile Point Beach. The beach forms the threshold of a pretty bay that wouldn't look out of place in National Geographic.

On your way back to the highway, stop at the bridge to have a look at a rocky chute where the Rosseau River thunders into Lake Rosseau each the spring. The torrent dries to a trickle during the summer. Peter Mutchenbacker managed a sawmill for the Snider Lumber Company at the river mouth. From 1905 to the early 1930s, the mill was run by Kaufman Furniture Ltd.

16 ROSSEAU RIVER RAPIDS

This pleasant picnic spot was once the site of the first public school in Cardwell Township. It was a board-and-batten structure erected in 1888. A second school, built in 1932, was located kitty-corner to this, across the river on the south side of the road. It closed in 1952 and is now used as a residence.

If, in your explorations here, you come across the huge deposit of sawdust in the bush, you'll have discovered the site of Albert Fry's sawmill. Fry managed the large mill at the mouth of the Rosseau River for the Kaufman Company of Kitchener. Fry moved to the highway (then called the Parry Sound Road) in 1936 and began his own sawmill operation. The mill operated until 1953, employing many local men.

Be prepared. There are a series of spectacular sights coming up. First a very steep hill and a rock face that threatens to crash down on you, then a lakeshore that comes up to your hubcaps, then more cliffs and a river. It's almost too much to take in.

17 SKELETON BAY/BENT RIVER

Thank goodness for modern roadbuilding techniques. You'd never see this cliff-face otherwise. The road to Bracebridge previously ran inland, over the top of the cliffs at the end of Skeleton Bay. The old road is still there, in fact, and used by hunters each fall. In places it's so steep you have to stop to catch your breath. In the early days, farmers planned to work their fields by the road in the summer months, hoping to make a few extra dollars pulling cars up the hill with their teams of horses.

Skeleton Bay conjures up images of mysterious bones being dredged from the water. In this case the bones weren't found here, but in nearby Skeleton Lake, which feeds this bay via the circuitous Skeleton River. The bends in the river account for the name of the nearby community, Bent River.

At the base of the cliffs stood Clement House (aka Granite Valley Lodge), a pioneer resort operated by Albert J. Clements. He purchased the property in 1892 and was instrumental in having the Parry Sound Road rerouted to come down to the bay and across their beach, bypassing the steep hill. The Clements moved the old Bent River school to their property in 1912 to serve as a staff

*Clement House,
Skeleton Bay. The road
now runs over the
Clement House beach.*
BENT RIVER
TWEEDSMUIR HISTORY

house. The Burton family purchased the lodge and changed the name to Burton Cliff Motel. Later it was called The Cliffs. In 1978, a group of investors purchased the property, which is now owned jointly by ten people.

18   SKELETON LAKE FISH HATCHERY PARK AND HIKING TRAIL

Distance: 1.2 kilometres (Turn left at Fish Hatchery Road)

Here's a spot you really must visit, simply to discover what rare treasures can be found if you get off the highway. A one-kilometre trail meanders along the picturesque river. Interpretative signs, placed by the Muskoka Heritage Foundation, describe points of interest along the way.

The Ministry of Natural Resources closed the fish hatchery in 1991. The Township later purchased the property and developed the park, with the assistance of local residents and students at Watt Public School. The late Aubrey Goltz, who spearheaded the effort to create this park, would be pleased with the result, with one exception: the fish ponds remain empty. It used to be quite an attraction to see the fingerlings jumping in the ponds.

Skeleton Lake is renowned for its clarity. Unique in Muskoka, the lake has a limestone bottom created as a result of an impact with a meteor. While the glaciers scoured nearly all the limestone in the Muskoka area, a thick pocket of the rock remained at the bottom of Skeleton Lake.

The Indians felt the lake had a certain power. Vernon Wadsworth, a man who helped with a land survey in the 1860s, asked the Indians the origin of the name: "They called it Spirit Lake for the reason that ghosts and spirits were there. They did not encamp there on this account, fearing to do so," he reported.

The surveyors did discover two skeletons: the bodies of an Indian mother and her son who died one winter when food was scarce.

A view through Madill Church.
PHOTO BY G.W. CAMPBELL

The R.M.S. Segwun *docked at Port Carling.*
PHOTO BY G.W. CAMPBELL

The falls at Bala.
PHOTO BY G.W. CAMPBELL

St. John the Baptist Church, Morinus.
PHOTO BY G.W. CAMPBELL

Shadow River, Rosseau.
PHOTO BY G.W. CAMPBELL

Hidden Valley, Peninsula Lake.
PHOTO BY G.W. CAMPBELL

Autumn at the Oxtongue Rapids.
PHOTO BY G.W. CAMPBELL

Hunter's Bridge, Oxtongue Rapids Park.
PHOTO BY G.W. CAMPBELL

Indian Landing, Port Sydney.
PHOTO BY G.W. CAMPBELL

Spring greens, Peninsula Lake.
PHOTO BY G.W. CAMPBELL

Watch for the Dee Bank Road sign and turn right. A short way along this road, the landscape changes from frowning cliffs to rolling farmlands. The soil in parts of the Three Mile Lake area is clay-based, generally deeper, heavier and more fertile than elsewhere in Muskoka. The clay plain is the result of silt deposits settling on the bottom of glacial Lake Algonquin thousands of years ago. The glacial lake collected the run-off from the retreating glaciers and covered most of Muskoka for about 900 years.

19 DEE BANK FALLS

After passing the Windermere Garden Centre, turn left onto North Shore Road. Not far from the corner, you'll spot the Dee River, tumbling down from Three Mile Lake.

The sound of rushing water drowns even the whisper of wind, here. Thick slabs of rock invite you to step down to the water's edge, maybe even paddle your feet in the water. This seemingly untouched setting was once home to a substantial grist mill and its companion sawmill in the 1870s. When John Shannon built the grist mill in 1871 it was the second such operation in the whole of Muskoka, the first being Bailey's grist mill at Bracebridge.

To the early settlers a flour mill of this sort was a godsend, and Dee Bank became an important community because of it. The school was located here, and a store and inn. As is often the case in Muskoka, the coming of the steamboats stole the spotlight from one community and focused it on another. Dee Bank's nemesis was Windermere, the port of call for the steamer *Waubamik* on its route from Port Carling to Rosseau.

20 WINDERMERE

No matter what modern events are shaping history, you will always find, at Windermere House, a wide, cool verandah; a dining room with crisp white tablecloths; grounds with herb gardens and hollyhocks; and a sunroom with tall windows and strong stone walls.

Like most of the early hotels, Windermere House started out as a modest family home, built by a Scotsman named Thomas Aitken around 1869. By this time sportsmen had discovered the area and Aitken's home became a rallying ground for hunting and fishing expeditions. In a little over a decade his home had become Windermere House.

By 1902–03, the hotel had doubled in size and sported two towers, a feature that characterized the building throughout the century. After Thomas's death in 1919, his son Leslie took over the resort. Ownership passed to Leslie's daughter, Mary Elizabeth, who ran the resort with the help of her aunt Gertrude and uncle Charles Roper, until 1981.

Waiting for the steamer at the Windermere wharf. The photo shows Windermere House as it looked after the addition of the second tower. MUSKOKA LAKES MUSEUM

A consortium of investors had just completed major improvements to the hotel when a fire destroyed it in February 1996, during the filming of an action movie, *The Long Kiss Goodnight*, starring Geena Davis. Determined to build a hotel that looked just like the old one, the Windermere Corporation undertook a massive construction project and opened the following year, May 31, 1997.

While Windermere House is the main attraction in the community, the village itself is worth exploring. Across from Windermere House stood the general store and post office (this building is being renovated as a family residence). Next to it stood the famous Windermere Dairy, operated by Thomas Aitken's grandson, Fred.

To the west, there's a heritage church tucked away in the spruce trees. Christ Church is over 90 years old. The rustic church has hand-decorated doors and expertly crafted stained-glass windows.

Adjoining the inn grounds is the Windermere Golf and Country Club, a professional course set in the gently rolling Windermere landscape, at one time prime sheep-grazing country. The reputation of Muskoka lamb made the Windermere farms famous.

Return to the Y-intersection and turn right on Windermere Road. A short drive brings you to the Brackenrig Road turnoff. This road travels fairly close to the Lake Rosseau shoreline, with its pleasant cottages and boxy wooden boathouses, packed like children's building blocks along the shore.

21 BRACKENRIG BAY

Turn right at Dock Road. At the end of the road, there's a small public wharf, owned by the Township of Muskoka Lakes.

Benjamin Hardcastle Johnston was the first to settle here with his sons, William, Robert, Benjamin and Garry, around 1866. From here Mr. Johnston visited the Indian Village at what is now Port Carling and decided to move there. He became Port Carling's postmaster in 1869. In spite of Mr. Johnston's departure, the community grew. The settlers had postal service (1876) and a one-room school.

22 PENNEY'S SAWMILL

Penney's sawmill, located on Penney's Road, contributed to the war effort during World War Two, when the navy needed lifeboats. The bow stems and seat braces from these boats were made from naturally curved pieces of wood, which were found where tree trunks joined tree roots.

The Penney Mill had the ideal setup for sawing whole tree trunks — roots and all — to produce a four-by-four piece of wood roughly shaped like an L. The boatbuilders then used a bandsaw to further shape the bow stems.

The mill operated seven days a week supplying the local boatbuilders and shipping as far away as Nova Scotia. They used tamarack because it was a suitable wood for salt water. Longtime Brackenrig resident and mill owner, Dudley Penney says the contractors had men in the swamps felling trees and digging the roots out of the ground. "They cleaned out all the swamps in a radius of 30 miles."

The mill's history dates back to 1918 when Thomas Rosseau Knight purchased the equipment new. He used the first lumber to form three sides and the roof of the mill, leaving one side open, as it is today. Dudley helped Mr. Knight with the sawing, and later bought the mill. Dudley's son. Ken Penney, now operates the mill.

Brackenrig Road continues past Brandy Lake to Muskoka Road 118, concluding the tour of Lake Rosseau.

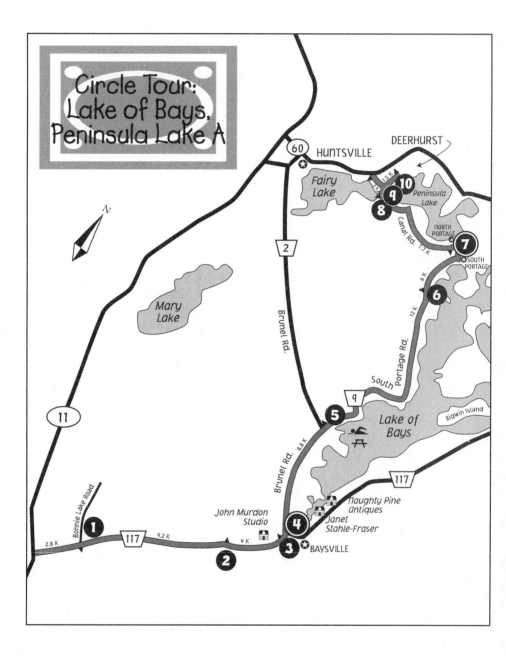

Circle Tour:
Lake of Bays,
Peninsula Lake A

60 HUNTSVILLE

DEERHURST

Fairy
Lake

1.5 K

Peninsula
Lake

10

9

8

NORTH
PORTAGE

Canal Rd. 7.7 K

7

SOUTH
PORTAGE

2

6 K

6

Brunel Rd.

12 K

Portage Rd.

Mary
Lake

11

South

9

Bigwin Island

5

Lake of
Bays

Brunel Rd. 8.8 K

117

Naughty Pine
Antiques

John Murdon
Studio

4

Janet
Stahle-Fraser

Bonnie Lake Road

1

117

4.2 K

4 K

3

BAYSVILLE

2.8 K

2

CHAPTER 5

Circle Tour: Lake of Bays and Peninsula Lake (A)

Baysville, North Portage, Canal Road
Distance: 54 kilometres (33 miles)

Starting at the intersection of Highway 11 and Muskoka Road 117, this tour takes you east to Baysville, then north along the west side of Lake of Bays.

As you drive east you leave the sandy soil and gravel deposits left by glacial run-off into prehistoric Lake Algonquin. The lake formed at the foot of the melting glaciers and covered most of Muskoka for 900 years. The drive to Baysville is punctuated with clumps of grey rock and steep ravines,

Lake of Bays is my favourite Muskoka lake. Not only are there plenty of opportunities to *see* the lake from the car, but places to get out and enjoy it. When you stop, you'll likely hear a loon in the distance. His plaintive cry reminds you that the lake, despite its popularity, is still delightfully wild. The route curves around 563 kilometres (350 miles) of shoreline — so steep in places, you wonder how the cottages manage to get a toehold.

Another intriguing aspect of the lake, is its legendary lake monster. While it may not be in the same league as the Loch Ness monster, it has, nonetheless, developed its own notoriety. Some think it is a survivor from prehistoric days; others think it's just a hoax, although there are documented reports of sightings.

In early days, steamboat travellers portaged between Lake of Bays and Peninsula Lake on a miniature locomotive called the Portage Railway. The tour takes you along the old rail line and across a canal to the famous Deerhurst Inn.

The following chapter completes the circle tour of Lake of Bays and Peninsula Lake by taking you down the eastern shorelines through Dwight and Dorset, returning to Baysville via Muskoka Road 117.

— Sights —

Old Macaulay Town Hall
Baysville Dam
Grindstone Memorial
Portage Railway Historic Site
Peninsula Lake Canal

— Antiques —

Cross Cut Antiques
Bridge Street
Baysville
705-767-2500

Naughty Pine Antiques
Muskoka Road 117
(just east of Baysville)
705-767-3114

— Arts and Crafts —

The Manse Gallery
Bay Street
Baysville
705-767-3117

John Murden Studio
Muskoka Road 117
(just west of Baysville)
705-767-2578

Janet Stahle-Fraser
Tapawingo Studio
Muskoka Road 117
(just east of Baysville)
705-767-3594
By appointment

The Village Croft
Bay Street
Baysville
705-767-2538

Wendy's Gifts and Things
Bay Street
Baysville
705-767-2181

POINTS OF INTEREST ON HIGHWAY 117

1   OLD MACAULAY TOWN HALL
Discussions on road maintenance and municipal taxes once filled the interior of this tiny town hall, built by the Township of Macaulay in 1885. It started its life facing Muskoka Road 117, but was turned the other way when the province widened the highway. While the Macaulay school was being built, students attended classes here for a short time. Nancy and Al Pratt, owners of the Bracebridge Golf Club, restored the old building, which was once used as an antique shop. The township was named after Chief Justice John B. Macaulay, a veteran of the War of 1812 who was active in public affairs.

2   OLD ROAD
An earlier road to Baysville ran a little to the south of the present one. You can see one of the old bridge abutments on the right-hand side. In the 1870s workmen hauled the steamer *Waubamik* ("white beaver") overland to Baysville along this route. Captain Huckins had purchased the steamer from A.P. Cockburn and planned to run it on Lake of Bays. At Bracebridge the *Waubamik* was hoisted onto a wagon and dragged along the road until it mired in the mud. Steve Fortin took over the laborious task and used a sled to pull the steamer to Baysville. In 1939 the steam yacht *Naiad* made the same journey when it was delivered to boat collector Cameron Peck.

The old road curved and twisted like a snake and had one steep section called the Devil's Gap. It was here, in 1874, that Bracebridge storekeeper Mr. Teviotdale and two ministers upset their vehicle, with Mr. Teviotdale landing underneath the other passengers. No one was hurt, but Mr. Teviotdale found he had a good story to tell by complaining that he'd nearly been smothered to death by two preachers in the Devil's Gap.

3   FAIRY FALLS ROAD
Fairy Falls Road is on the right-hand side as you enter Baysville. It was named after an early settler, Thomas Fairy, who settled at the falls in 1873. In 1891, while he and his son were working in the field, a fire destroyed his home. His wife tried to put out the fire and, failing at that, tried to rescue the family's belongings. She was badly burned and died shortly afterwards.

After Fairy Falls Road you'll soon see Brunel Road (Muskoka Road 2) leading off Muskoka Road 117 on the left. This takes you up the west side of Lake of Bays, where the tour continues after a stop in Baysville.

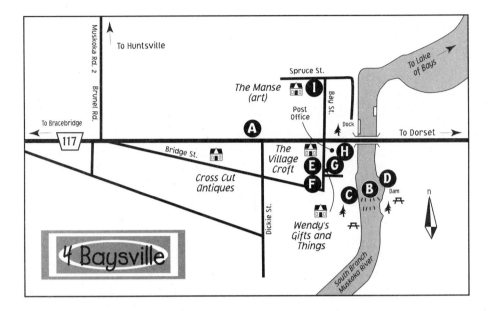

4   BAYSVILLE

Baysville is a leafy, compact village. There are many historic sites, all within a stone's throw of each other, plus shady streets and interesting shops. Mark Langford was the first settler to journey this way in 1870. He cut a path through the bush to locate the free land grant his father had claimed. When Langford found the lot, he decided the land was too difficult to tame — especially for his father, who was handicapped. Thomas Langford stubbornly refused to listen to his son and moved his family to the area outside Baysville in 1871.

That same year William H. Brown located on land that is now the village. The government agreed to give Brown extra land and water rights at the falls if Brown reciprocated by building a sawmill. Brown had the village site surveyed and gave land for three churches and the school.

Baysville became a major logging centre with at least seven hotels for boarding loggers. Pictures from the 1890s show the Mickle-Dyment Lumber Company yards on the west side of the Muskoka River stretching from the present bridge site to the dam. Other lumber companies, such as Shier, Robert Dollar, and Rathbun, joined with Mickle-Dyment to form a boom company and build a dam to raise the water level between Lake of Bays and the south branch of the Muskoka River.

The Archeological and Historic Sites Board of Ontario has erected two plaques in the village. One commemorates the explorers of Muskoka and Haliburton; another recognizes William Brown as founder of the settlement.

Historic plaque tells the explorers' story, at the Baysville dam. PHOTO BY SUSAN PRYKE

4A SCHOOLHOUSE HILL

As you come into Baysville, you'll see a rocky hill where St. Ambrose Anglican Church watches over the village. The wooden building beside the church was the original schoolhouse in Baysville and dates back to 1874-75. Local residents call this rock "schoolhouse hill." When St. Ambrose church burned in 1919, parishioners moved the school here and used it for church services. The predecessor of the brick church (consecrated in 1922) was a similarly shaped wooden structure dedicated to St. Ambrose of Milan.

Across the way, Bethune United Church, on Dickie Street, dates to 1883. It takes its name from a Christian student, Mr. Bethune, who instigated the building of the church. Mr. Bethune later became the father or Dr. Norman Bethune (see Chapter 2).

In early days, St. Ambrose was on a quiet side street. The main thoroughfare into Baysville was Bridge Street, so named because the first bridge crossed the river at the foot of the street, near Brown's sawmill.

St. Ambrose Church.
PHOTO BY SUSAN PRYKE

Baysville dam. PHOTO BY SUSAN PRYKE

4B BAYSVILLE DAM

Lumber companies took a keen interest in water levels along the south branch of the Muskoka River and formed a consortium, called a boom company, to construct a wooden dam in 1872. In the days before the dam, the water was so shallow that ladies could walk across the exposed river stones in their canvas shoes in the summer.

In 1918, the Department of Public Works built a picturesque stone dam with three gates. Contractors replaced this dam with the modern cement structure your see today. A pamphlet printed for the opening of the dam on 20 July, 1960 published the names of the officials present that day: R.J. Boyer, MPP for Muskoka; the Hon. Ray Connel, Minister of Public Works; and the Hon. Leslie M. Frost, Premier of Ontario.

During the Second World War several Baysville veterans took turns guarding the dam. It seems the government was concerned about plots to sabotage the Baysville dam and disrupt power schemes farther down the river. Viola Vanclieaf remembers the veterans, in official uniform, marching back and forth across the dam.

4C BAYSVILLE SAWMILL

William Brown, the founder of Baysville, built a sawmill on the west side of the dam in 1873. Today the site is surrounded by a park, which looks out at the gentle rapids below the dam. If you look carefully you can see remains of the mill's foundations in the rocks.

Brown's sawmill. W.H. Brown built the first dam on the river in 1872. The sawmill, seen on the left, dates to 1873.
ONTARIO ARCHIVES 2839

4D BAYSVILLE GRIST MILL

Bill Gammage built a grist mill on the opposite side of the dam in 1877. He also operated a store where settlers could exchange grain for provisions. The grindstones from the Gammage mill are on display at the cenotaph park.

4E WILLIAM BROWN'S HOUSE (Burtons' Bed and Breakfast)

Baysville's founder, William Brown, built the first brick house in the community in 1872. Today his great-granddaughter, Shirley Burton, and her husband Bob operate a bed and breakfast in the historic home. Oxen carried the bricks all the way from Washago. More were hauled from Dorset in a birchbark canoe. The front door and much of the window glass is original. The wood trim came from William Brown's sawmill. The lamps at the front of the house are from a stagecoach that ran between Baysville and Bracebridge.

Baysville's first post office opened in William Brown's kitchen in 1873. They say Mrs. Brown, the assistant postmaster, kept letters in her sewing machine drawer. The house was also used for religious services before the churches were built.

William Brown's House.
PHOTO BY SUSAN PRYKE

Baysville House and hunters. Today the building is called The Rock. BAYSVILLE TWEEDSMUIR HISTORY

4F BAYSVILLE HOUSE

James. R. Smith built Baysville House sometime in the 1870s to cater to the growing number of lumbermen in the area. The building changed hands many times before being purchased by Robert Lincoln Menzies in 1946. His daughter, Betty Maynard, ran the hotel until recently, under the name her father had given it, Lincoln Lodge. Today it is called The Rock Restaurant and Tavern.

4G LANGMAID'S STORE (dates to 1873)

Captain G.F. Marsh — of whom you'll hear more in the following pages — began his Muskoka enterprises in the Langmaid Store location in the 1870s. The Baysville Tweedsmuir History says he acquired a steamboat from Captain Wilkins and began trading on Lake of Bays. He also dabbled in the lumber business and had a wharf and storehouse behind his home.

In the early 1920s, William Langmaid moved his grocery store to this location, taking over from previous owners who had run a supply store for the loggers. Langmaid also operated a butcher's shop and a supply boat, which carried goods to residents around Lake of Bays.

The store, as you see it, is pretty much as it was in Langmaid's day. The U-shaped counter has been chopped away to make room for displays. Also gone is the woodstove that sat in the middle of the room. The store is now a gift and antique shop called Wendy's Gifts and Things.

Grindstone Memorial, Baysville.
PHOTO BY G.W. CAMPBELL

4H GRINDSTONE MEMORIAL

The grindstones from Bill Gammage's mill have been incorporated into a memorial park honouring Baysville veterans. The park marks the location of the old Pulford House, built in 1906 when the township of McLean voted "dry" in a temperance referendum. Alexander Judson Henderson built the hotel because the other hoteliers in the area threatened to "pull up stakes" after the temperance vote. As it turned out, they did not leave town so Henderson, faced with continued competition, decided to operate the hotel in the summer months only. J.J. Robertson purchased the hotel in 1922 and changed the name to the Robertson Inn. The hotel was known as Riverside when it burned in 1940. Investigators found that wires had overheated and started a fire in the linen closet.

4-I THE MANSE GALLERY

The Manse Gallery dates to the early 1900s. In 1918 the United Church purchased the building as a rectory for pastors of Bethune United Church. Shirley Prittie and Carole Young have transformed the old building into a charming gallery, which operates daily throughout the summer and on weekends from 24 May through to Thanksgiving.

The tour continues up the western shoreline of Lake of Bays. You'll have to backtrack a bit to Brunel Road, at the western entrance to Baysville, and turn right. The next stretch of the journey is perfect for Sunday drivers — just sit back and soak up the scenery.

Brunel Road rolls over hills, past Tooke and Schufelt lakes, to the South Portage Road (Muskoka Road 9). Turn right and watch for the Lake of Bays Park.

5   LAKE OF BAYS PICNIC SPOT

The old saying "good things come in small packages" aptly describes this mini picnic spot under the cedar trees. I like to eat my lunch on the dock and paddle my feet. There's something about the water of Lake of Bays that tempts you to dive in. I expect even non-swimmers feel the urge to wade when confronted with these shallow, sparkling waters.

— Lake of Bays — Lake of Many Names —

When Lieutenant Henry Briscoe travelled across Lake of Bays in 1826 he called it Baptiste Lake. Lieutenant F. H. Baddeley did not actually see Lake of Bays on his 1835 expedition, but his Indian guide spoke of the lake and called it Nagatoagoman. No translation of that name was given.

David Thompson passed this way during his 1837 expedition. At that time he reported another Indian name, Nun-ge-low-e-nee-goo Mark-so-lak-a-hagan, which means "the Lake of the Forks from its many Deep Bays and Points of Land." Thompson wisely shortened the translation to Forked Lake.

In 1829 Alexander Shirreff discovered remains of trading posts around the shores, especially in the Bigwin Island area. His name, Trading Lake, survived for many years and is still used to refer to the bay beyond the narrows at Dorset.

Alexander Murray coined the name Lake of Bays in his 1853 geological survey of the area. Although settlers seemed to prefer the name Trading Lake, Lake of Bays was popularized by tourism pamphlets put out by the Grand Trunk Railway.

6. MAHARISHI INTERNATIONAL ACADEMY
   OF THE SCIENCE OF CREATIVE INTELLIGENCE (Britannia Hotel)

The sign for this centre for transcendental meditation catches you off guard on your journeys through Muskoka. When you think of it, though, what better place to get in touch with your inner self than the calm surroundings of a lakeside resort? The Maharishi Academy comprises the former Britannia Hotel site, a famous luxury resort operated by Thomas J. White from 1908 onwards. Bigwin Inn's designer, John Wilson, drew up the plans for Britannia, which featured a gambrel roof and huge balconies. Thomas White had spotted the property on a canoe trip in 1901 and purchased it. From 1955-57, White's son, Paul, converted the resort into a year-round operation with a curling rink, ski trails and ski lift. He tore down the old hotel and built a modern, all-season building, which is still being used today.

White sold the resort to a consortium of former guests, who later sold it to the present owners. The bush has begun reclaiming the fairways and ski hills, obliterating the manicured grounds of a former era. The road to the lake is a private one, although older maps show this as the way to the community of Kingsway. A post office of that name operated at the Britannia Hotel. Thomas White's wife came across the name on a trip to England.

About three kilometres past the Maharishi Academy, you come to the landing at South Portage and, across from it, North Portage Road, which takes you to North Portage.

7   PORTAGE RAILWAY — THE SMALLEST RAILWAY IN THE WORLD

Today the landing at South Portage is a quiet docking place where visitors can gaze out at the water, fish or have a picnic. On occasion a bevy of mallard ducks will drift by the boat-launching ramp looking for handouts.

This idyllic calm belies the bustling activity of the early days when steamboats and private launches jockeyed for position at the crowded dockside. Piles of tanbark and lumber littered the shoreline. Chugging amongst the steamboats and the precarious piles of freight was the Portage Train, Muskoka's own "Little Engine That Could."

To understand the history of the portage railway and its links with navigation on Peninsula Lake (to the north) and Lake of Bays (to the south), you must go back to the 1890s when the bridge of land now traversed by North Portage Road was the only bottleneck to a completely integrated transportation system on the north Muskoka lakes.

In 1875 a lock on the north branch of the Muskoka River linked navigation on Mary, Fairy and Vernon lakes. Peninsula Lake joined the trio in

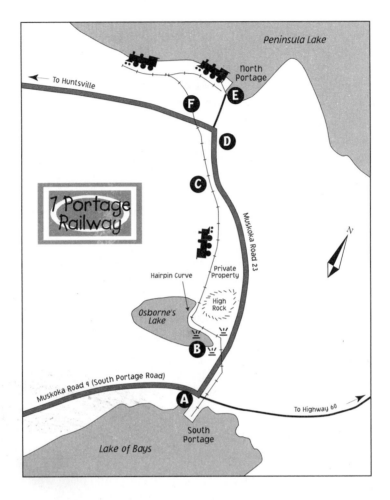

Peninsula Lake

To Huntsville

North Portage

E

F

D

7 Portage Railway

C

Muskoka Road 23

Hairpin Curve

Private Property

Osborne's Lake

High Rock

B

N

Muskoka Road 9 (South Portage Road)

A

To Highway 60

South Portage

Lake of Bays

1888 when a dredging machine cut a canal through from Fairy to Peninsula Lake. Being 31 metres (100 feet) higher than Peninsula Lake, Lake of Bays was not an easy piece to fit into the transportation picture.

Although the distance between the lakes was just one mile, the cost of linking Peninsula and Lake of Bays by water (with two locks and a canal) was exorbitant. Instead contractors built a gravel road across the portage and a local family, the Osbornes, hauled passengers and freight across in a wagon.

Travelling by water was the only way to get anywhere in comfort in those days. With that knowledge in mind, Captain G.F. Marsh and Captain Denton battled it out for the steamboat monopoly on the north Muskoka lakes. In the end, Marsh succeeded. He formed the Huntsville and Lake of Bays Transportation Company in 1895 and began looking for ways to smooth out the transportation bottleneck at the portage.

It was his idea to build a railway across the portage. In 1903 workers began putting down tracks for the world's smallest railway. Marsh, who was suffering from cancer at the time, lived long enough to take one trip on the train several months after it started to operate in 1904.

C.O. Shaw, general manager of the Anglo-Canadian Leather Company in Huntsville, took over the steamboat and railway system, which he ran in conjunction with a luxury resort called Bigwin Inn on Lake of Bays. Control of Shaw's Huntsville and Lake of Bays Navigation Company passed to his daughter Pauline Gill after Shaw's death in 1942 and to her son-in-law, Carl McLennan in 1948.

Owing to the steep incline of the portage and the shortness of the run, the little train ran backward (with the engine pushing the cars) from a switch at the north end of the route to the South Portage wharf, and forward from South Portage to the switch at the north end. The seats in the two passenger cars swivelled, allowing passengers to see where they were going at all times.

The train was an endearing little thing, but it worked hard. Some old railroad hands don't take kindly to teasing remarks about the Portage Flyer or the Hot Tamale Express. But there's no escaping the fact that on the uphill run people could jump off the train and pick a few strawberries if they felt like it.

Travelling on the Portage train was a little like climbing aboard an amusement-park ride, especially as it squealed round Osborne Lake with the edges of the cars hanging over the shoreline.

Steamers at the South Portage wharf, Lake of Bays.

When the Navigation Company pulled its last boat off the north Muskoka lakes' run in 1958, the Portage Railway ran for one more year as a tourist attraction. Then the rails were dismantled and the rolling stock sold to a theme park in St. Thomas, Ontario.

The good new is this: the Portage Train has returned to Muskoka, thanks to the efforts of a group of volunteers, including the Huntsville and Lake of Bays Railway Society. By the year 2000 they hope to have the rail bed laid from one end of Huntsville's Pioneer Village to Fairy Lake so the Portage Flyer can carry passengers as it once did, albeit in a new location.

7A SOUTH PORTAGE

The landfilled South Portage wharf covers the remains of the steamboat *Iroquois*, which sank at the old wharf in the winter of 1949. The *Iroquois* was a pretty steamboat built in 1906 to ply between South Portage and Dorset. When it sank, the owners took out all usable material and left the stripped hull at the side of the dock. Today the remains are covered with landfill (although you can see parts of the boat in the water). The *Iroquois'* replacement, the *Iroquois II*, was a modern launch that had neither the style nor the capacity of the old steamer.

A line of evergreen trees along North Portage Road marks the path the railway took down to the wharf. The tracks went right to the end of the dock. In later years, the owners built a roof over the last section of the line to protect both the passengers and the train from the weather.

7B OSBORNE'S (or Little) LAKE

As you start over the portage along North Portage Road, you'll notice a marshy section on the left. In autumn, when the leaves have fallen, you can actually glimpse Osborne's Lake behind the alders. At this point the rail line travelled away from the present road, along the shores of the lake.

7C RAILWAY EMBANKMENT

After you've crested the hill and are two-thirds of the way down the other side, look to your left for the old Portage Railway embankment, which has been cleared for a snowmobile trail. The remains of a cinder rail bed and rotting rail ties are the only evidence that the railway existed.

7D PORTAGE INN

Before Captain Marsh built the "world's shortest rail line" between Peninsula Lake and Lake of Bays, a horse-drawn wagon carried passengers over the portage. At that time, someone decided it made good sense to put up a hotel along the route. Originally built by J.G. Henderson in 1889, the modest

Portage train at Osborne's Lake. MUSKOKA LAKES MUSEUM

Lake View hotel sat on a gentle slope overlooking Peninsula Lake. The arrival of the railway was not necessarily seen as a godsend, because stray embers from the smokestack of the Portage Flyer occasionally set fire to the grass and the building itself. The named changed to Hotel La Portage, then Portage Lodge. By the 1940s the Walker family ran the hotel, which was renowned for its fine spring water.

From the 1960s onwards, the hotel had a hard time staying in business and was finally sold to John Turner, who turned it into a disco called Portage Station. This name led to the mistaken belief that the building was somehow connected to the railway operations.

In the mid 1980s, Cathy Sloan converted the inn into a health retreat for women and operated it successfully for several years. After being vacant for a few years, the inn is back in business as a year-round bed and breakfast operation.

7E NORTH PORTAGE

A private dock has replaced the old North Portage wharf, but you can still find remnants of rail ties in the grass along the shore, where the line ran to the switch. From the switch, the train backed up the incline. A group of cottages, including some modern duplexes, sits on the site where the North Portage store and post office once stood. The Hood family operated the store in the early years, followed by the Waltons and the Thompsons.

S.S. Algonquin *and yacht* Sarona *at the canal.* PHOTO COURTESY IAN TURNBULL

7F   RAILWAY RIGHT OF WAY

Just past the Portage Inn corner, on Canal Road, you'll see where the Portage Railway line ran through the bush. The right of way has not yet grown over completely.

8   CANAL COMMUNITY SCHOOL

Just before the road crosses the bridge over the canal, you'll notice a charming red brick house. This little building has the distinction of being one of the few former schoolhouses in Muskoka to have had three names. Because the school served three townships, officials called it SS #8 Brunel, SS #11 Chaffey and SS #7 Franklin. The brick school opened in 1927 and continued to operate until 1941 when low attendance closed the school temporarily. In 1947 it reopened and stayed open for another ten years.

Prior to the construction of the brick school, children attended classes in a small white church that sat on the banks of the canal. The church was moved in recent years to allow construction of a new bridge over the canal.

9   PENINSULA CANAL

Prior to the construction of the canal, a small creek flowed through this gap from Peninsula Lake to Fairy Lake. A difference in water levels of 38 centimetres (15 inches) brought some concerns about tampering with natural water levels, but local settlers were eager to join the established navigation system linking Mary, Fairy and Vernon lakes. Dredging began in 1886 and the canal opened two years later.

Deerhurst Resort, 1925. PHOTO COURTESY IAN TURNBULL

10 DEERHURST INN

(Distance: 1.7 kilometres)

To the right, off Canal Road, are the expansive grounds of Deerhurst Resort. This world-class resort began as a wilderness retreat accessible only by steamboat. The inn's founder, Charles Waterhouse, built the resort in 1896. In those days the northern Muskoka lakes were not as well known as they are today. In fact, that first summer Mr. Waterhouse entertained a total of two guests. By 1899, however, he had to turn visitors away.

Like its namesake, a grand estate in England, Deerhurst Inn cultivated a relaxed, genteel atmosphere. Gentlemen clustered in the smoking room to discuss hunting and fishing while women strolled across the grounds under layers of white muslin and broad-brimmed hats.

From 1923 to 1971, Deerhurst's reputation grew under the direction of Charles' son, Maurice. Bill Waterhouse, Maurice's son, took over in 1971. When Bill sold his interest in the resort in 1989, the inn had become a winterized resort with conference facilities that could accommodate more than 1,000 people. In 1998, New Castle Hotels took over management of the hotel, which now offers condominium-style accommodation and two 18-hole golf courses. The new sports pavilion is a popular venue for conferences, entertainment extravaganzas and sporting functions.

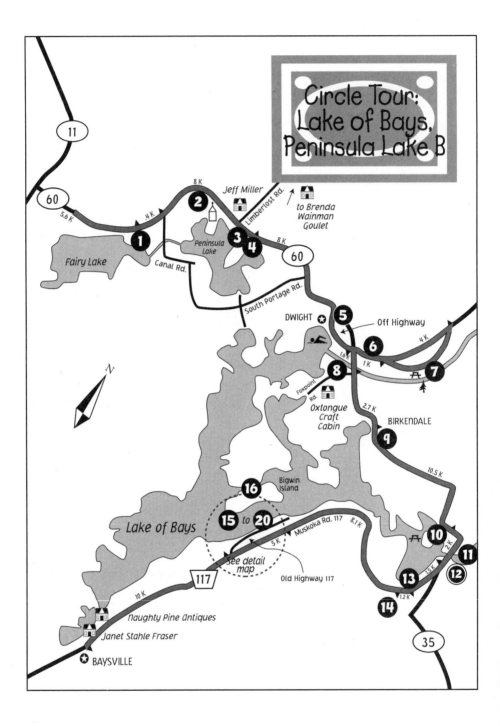

Circle Tour:
Lake of Bays,
Peninsula Lake B

CHAPTER 6

Circle Tour: Lake of Bays and Peninsula Lake (B)

Dwight, Dorset, Norway Point
Distance: 60 kilometres (37 miles)

It's no exaggeration to say this route is one of Muskoka's most spectacular autumn-colour tours. The combination of steep hills and deep rock cuts accentuates the splash of colour, which reaches a peak between the last week of September and the second week of October.

Some of the hills dive straight into Lake of Bays, others plunge into long, sandy beaches that are almost tropical. The best beaches are found at Norway Point, where the ill-fated WaWa hotel used to be. The resort was such a landmark that the Public Works Department had to moderate the height of water held behind the Baysville dam so as not to drown out any more of the sand beach than absolutely necessary.

This tour has a little bit of everything: rapids, waterfalls, romance and history. There are excellent lake views along the way, plus a tower lookout that takes you to dizzying heights above Lake of Bays.

— Sights —

Fairy Vista Trail
Dwight Bay Beach
Oxtongue Rapids
Marsh's Falls
Birkendale Rock Cut
Dorset Lookout Tower
Lake of Bays Park
WaWa Hotel Spring House
   (Historic Marker)
Bigwin Island

— Antiques —

Naughty Pine Antiques
Just east of Baysville
705-767-3114

— Arts and Crafts —

Jeff Miller (painter)
Limberlost Road
Dwight
705-635-2754
By chance or appointment

Brenda Wainman Goulet
(bronze sculptures)
Upper Walker Lake Road
(Off Limberlost Road)
Dwight
705-635-1996
By chance or appointment

Whippletree North
Highway 60
Dwight
705-635-9376

Oxtongue Craft Cabin/Gallery
Foxpoint Road
Dwight
705-635-1602

Greenaway Gallery
Main Street
Dorset
705-766-0242

Janet Stahle-Fraser
(hand-pulled original prints)
Tapawingo Studio
Muskoka Road 117
(just east of Baysville)
705-767-3594
By appointment

1   GRANDVIEW INN

This classic Muskoka inn started as an idea in the mind of a very determined woman, Minnie (Pleace) Cookson. Minnie was one of the legion of orphaned children from Britain who were selected by bush farmers in Canada and made to endure long days of heavy labour. She ran away from her placement and was taken in by a kind family in Huntsville.

She later met and married John Cookson, and set in motion her plans to build a summer hotel — even though her husband was not keen on the idea. She persevered and in 1911 Grandview opened for business. Advertised as the inn with the million dollar view, Grandview thrived. Minnie bolstered the inn's reputation with her fine cooking. All the vegetables, cream, milk, berries, lamb and chicken came from the family's 650-acre farm. The Cookson family continued to operate Grandview Inn until 1970, when Bruce and Judy Craik purchased the resort and started some major renovation work. The inn reopened in 1972.

The Evans family ran the resort from 1986–1998 when they sold the operation to ClubLink Corporation. Today the inn has earned a reputation as a vacation retreat that values outdoor pursuits such as hiking, birdwatching, nature tours and wilderness adventures.

Robert Ballantine
PHOTO COURTESY BARB PATERSON

Rev. Robert Norton Hill
PHOTO COURTESY BARB PATERSON

PENINSULA LAKE
AND ITS NORTH SHORE COMMUNITIES

While conducting a geological survey of the Muskoka area in 1853, Alexander Murray named several lakes in the district, including Peninsula Lake. Two peninsulas predominate the north shoreline marking the locations of two pioneers: Rev. R.N. Hill and Robert Ballantine.

Rev. Hill was the first to homestead in the area, selecting land in 1867. The community of Hillside began as a family settlement on the most easterly peninsula. In 1870 Robert Ballantine built a log cabin on the westerly peninsula, where the community of Grassmere took root. A rivalry developed between the two patriarchs as they tried to secure the prominence of their respective communities on the north shore of Peninsula Lake.

2   GRASSMERE

As more settlers arrived on Peninsula Lake, Robert Ballantine decided to set up a grist mill on the creek that bears his name. He built the mill in 1873. The following year he was appointed postmaster of the Grassmere post office, located in his home. A postal official thought the area looked like a valley in England called Grassmere, and suggested the name.

Grist mills in Port Sydney and Huntsville eventually put Ballantine's mill out of business. Robert died in 1892. His sons operated the business for a few more years. The mill was later dismantled and the material used to build a new house where Robert's widow, Mary(and later his daughter) ran the post office.

Today, Highway 60 bypasses the Grassmere post office, but the name Grassmere lives on in identifying the road which gives access to Cedar Grove and Pow-Wow Point resorts.

The small red brick church that you see from the highway is St. Paul's, which dates back to 1881, when a local settler donated land for the church. The church was dedicated in 1891.

3   TALLY HO LODGE

The grounds at the present Tally Ho resort were once Native encampments. Artifacts, including arrowheads and skinning stones, were uncovered regularly when Hugh Hill (grandson of Rev. R. N. Hill) plowed the fields. The Robinsons operated the first inn on the site, called Wequash ("white duck"). Gordon Hill, founder of nearby Limberlost resort, changed the name to Tally Ho when he purchased the property. Betty and Isabel Emberson bought Tally Ho in 1939. The inn was frequented by aspiring artists whose work can still be seen on the walls of the hotel.

4   HILLSIDE PIONEER MEMORIAL UNITED CHURCH

Hillside is named after Rev. Robert Norton Hill, who is said to have dreamed of this peninsula before finding it in 1867. He heard about the free land grants in Muskoka while attending a Methodist conference in Toronto, and came to see first hand what all the fuss was about. After investigating several parcels, Hill selected land at Fairy Lake. But that night he dreamed of a sweep of land jutting into the water, with an island in front of it. The next morning he set out on further explorations. When he discovered a location similar to the land he'd seen in his dreams, he knew it was meant for him. Hill's sons cleared the land in 1868. The next year Rev. Hill moved the family to the site — blazing a trail which eventually became Highway 60.

When Robert Ballantine secured a post office for his community, just a few miles away, in 1874, Hill was determined that his community should have a post office, too. In 1878, the Hillside post office opened in Rev. Hill's home. It was closed the next year when an informant (guess who?) told the Postmaster General that money was being wasted having two post offices so close together. Eventually the government allowed the Hillside post office to reopen in 1898.

The first church services in Hillside were conducted in the Hillside Public School, built in 1875. Rev. Hill also paddled across Peninsula and Fairy lakes to take services in the home of Capt. George Hunt, the founder of Huntsville.

By 1892, the Hillside settlers had built a Methodist church across the road from the school. Rev. Hill died a few years later (1895) and is lovingly remembered in the century-old Pioneer Memorial Church. The altar window is a memorial to the Hill family and the other pioneers in the Hillside community. Hill's 1874 home is restored and in use at the Muskoka Pioneer Village (see Chapter 7).

5   DWIGHT

Before echoing the name of its major benefactor, H.P. Dwight of the Great North Western Telegraph company, this area was referred to as North Bay. H.P. Dwight and his associate, Erastus Wiman, had been coming to Muskoka on fishing trips since 1863. On their first trip they ventured as far as Baysville, but did not go on to Lake of Bays because it seemed so wild and obscure.

View of Dwight, 1900. The little white building on the right is St. Peter's Presbyterian Church; behind it is the Dwight School. The boxlike Gouldie Manor is the most prominent building in the photograph. PHOTO COURTESY OF RHETA ASBURY, DWIGHT

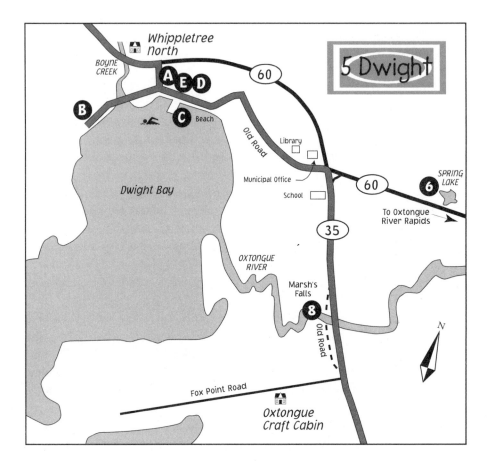

A decade passed and settlers eventually penetrated the area that these early fishermen said would need "great nerve and special outfit" to visit. Mr. Edmund J. Gouldie paddled into North Bay from Dorset in 1871. His nearest neighbour at that time was Mr. Tom Salmon at Fox Point. Salmon, Gouldie and another pioneer, Mr. Frank Blackwell, acted as guides for members of the Dwight-Wiman Hunt Club, who used Gouldie's house as their base of operations. Dwight found the area so much to his liking that he decided to set up a permanent hunting camp. Local settlers showed him land on Long Lake, several kilometres from Gouldie's, where he built a hunting lodge (circa 1884).

Meanwhile H.P. Dwight had become the president of the telegraph company. To keep in touch with his office, Dwight had a telegraph line run in to Gouldie's. Whenever company officials wished to contact their president they'd "send a telegram to Dwight." As more and more telegrams got sent to Dwight, his name became the "handle" that identified the community. The good citizens made it official in the naming of a post office in 1885. In later years H.P. Dwight donated money for the building of schools in the area and established libraries at Dwight and Dorset. He also sent gifts to the schools each Christmas.

Turn right at Dwight Bay Road to go down to the public beach and town wharf.

5A SITE OF THE FORMER SCHOOL AND MUNICIPAL BUILDING
The Lake of Bays municipal office, which sat next to the post office, burned on November 26, 1996. In its earlier life it had been the Dwight school. In 1956 students transferred to Irwin Memorial Central School. The Lake of Bays office has been rebuilt at the corner of Dwight Beach Road and Highway 60, by the Dwight library. It opened in February 1998.

5B STEWART MEMORIAL CHURCH
Stewart Memorial Church, built in 1887, is a testament to the Stewart family, who founded and cared for the church over the years. Rev. Alexander Stewart helped organize many frontier churches in the Grey-Bruce area and here in Muskoka. Stewart came to Dwight on the invitation of the Wilder and Wood families, who had been parishioners in his Durham Baptist Church before moving to Muskoka. He was 70 when he arrived in this area and purchased a bit of land for $40 near Boyne Creek. He travelled by horseback or foot to preach in homes around the area. Later he organized the Baptist Church, which was built near his home. His son, Rev. Joseph Stewart, took charge of summer services at that time and continued to do so for 50 years. When the little church came under the care of the United Church ministry in 1936, residents asked that it be renamed Stewart Memorial Church. It is the oldest building still standing in Dwight.

5C DWIGHT BAY BEACH
Dwight Bay beach is one of the most "walkable" stretches of shoreline in Muskoka. Long, sandy and gently curved, it crowns a placid bay that opens onto a horizon of high, wooded hills.

5D SITE OF EDMUND GOULDIE'S FIRST HOME
The Gouldie family owned all the land around Dwight Bay in the early days. Edmund Gouldie, the first settler, built his home on the site of the present Logging Chain Lodge. He opened a general store, post office and the first boarding house. A log school building, the predecessor of the frame school, was located by the lake in front of Edmund Gouldie's home.

Gouldie House, Dwight. LILY KIRKPATRICK COLLECTION

5E GOULDIE MANOR SITE

Archie Gouldie settled next door to his brother Edmund. As more and more sportsmen arrived, Archie Gouldie opened his home to tourists and by 1906 had enlarged it to accommodate up to 80 guests. Gouldie Manor, later known as Northland Lodge, eventually burned.

The Beach Road is the original road through the area. If you follow it, you'll rejoin Highway 60 near a Y-intersection. The main tour continues south along Highway 35, but you may wish to take a quick side trip north to see the wild rapids along the Oxtongue River.

SIDE TRIP TO OXTONGUE RIVER RAPIDS (Distance: 5 kilometres)

6   SPRING LAKE

Follow Highway 60 as it swings left towards Algonquin Park. On the left you'll glimpse Spring Lake, a kettle lake formed when a chunk of the retreating glacier became detached from the main ice sheet. Glaciers advanced and retreated at least four times during the Pleistocene Epoch. The last glacier released its icy grip on the area some 12,000 years ago. At Spring Lake an ice block became isolated in the sandy delta of the meltwater channel. Beached like a whale, the ice block melted and left a depression and a lake-sized puddle.

7 OXTONGUE RAPIDS PARK AND HUNTER'S BRIDGE

Two kilometres from the intersection of Highway 60 and Highway 35 turn right on the Oxtongue Rapids Park Road. The road cuts through sandy banks, which are the remains of deltas left by the precursor of the Oxtongue River. Earlier in its history the Oxtongue was swollen with the waters of a glacier as it retreated across the Algonquin Park dome.

I'll warn you the road is little more than a sandy track and you'll wonder if there is indeed a park hidden among the pines. Have patience and you'll reach the Lion's Club Park. From this point onwards there are several stopping-off places with picnic tables overlooking the river.

The Oxtongue is a troubled river that churns and boils angrily through rock clefts. The rapids stretch for 3.2 kilometres (about two miles) — very exhilarating for white-water canoeists.

HUNTER'S BRIDGE

Farther along the road, there's a cairn erected by the Dwight Lion's Club in memory of Lloyd Bradley and Ralph Blackwell, whose vision and efforts contributed to the reality of Oxtongue Rapids Park and Hunter's Bridge.

Hunter's Bridge is just below the cairn. There's a short, steep gravel road leading down to it, which might be washed out in sections if there's been heavy rain. At the bottom is the cantilever footbridge marking the end of the Bobcaygeon Road, where pioneer Isaac Hunter settled in the 1860s. It is thought that Hunter had something to do with the 1837 Rebellion (a citizens' revolt against the government), and that he came to the Dorset area to flee prosecution. As more people arrived, Hunter retreated to the very limits of the Bobcaygeon Road and here he died during a severe winter.

His body was found by Zac Cole, whom you'll meet in later chapters. Cole snowshoed to Hunter's cabin on a trip back from Algonquin Park. There he made a grisly discovery: Hunter's starved body was being devoured by mice, which his wife and daughter, on the fringe of lunacy, were trying to catch for food.

The Bobcaygeon colonization road was to run from Bobcaygeon to North Bay. Workmen began building the road in 1856. By 1863 construction was complete to the Oxtongue River, but abandoned near Hunter's Bridge. Later a sideroad linked the Bobcaygeon and Muskoka roads via the eastern shores of Fairy Lake, Peninsula Lake and Lake of Bays (more or less the route taken by today's Highway 60).

Turn left onto Highway 60 and return to the junction of Highways 60 and 35 at the Beacon Service Station. Continue on Highway 35. Grieves Robson built the first road to Dorset from Dwight sometime after 1883. The settlers called it Bull's Run, which gives you an idea of the comfort and smoothness of the roads in early days.

During the Depression, in the 1930s, the provincial government started a make-work project called the Northern Development Company. The company employed men who were "on relief" in the cities to build roads. The workers received $10 a month and all their meals. Road camps sprang up like tent cities at Marsh's Falls and Goose Lake along the present Highway 35.

8   MARSH'S FALLS

At Marsh's Falls the water flows like liquid glass from the base of the old bridge abutment, then whips into foam as it beats against the rocks. The Oxtongue River expends its last bit of wild energy on this obstacle and flows gently on to the lake.

Captain Marsh began his Muskoka enterprises in Baysville, where he dabbled in lumbering and farming. By 1878 Marsh had moved to the falls on the Oxtongue River. At the beach, on the north side of the river, Marsh built the *Mary Louise*, the first of his fleet of steamboats. On the opposite shore, he built a transportation depot. Here passengers embarked from the *Mary Louise* and boarded a stage that ran to Oxtongue Lake.

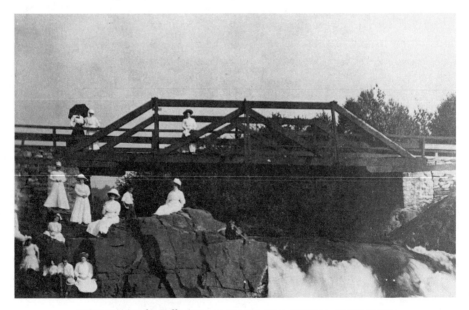

Picnic at Marsh's Falls. PHOTO COURTESY OF L.G. CRAWFORD, NORWAY POINT

While in this location, Marsh ran his steamboat in competition with Captain Huckins' *Excelsior* out of Baysville. Each captain tried to undercut the other's prices, and you could say Marsh drove Huckins out of business. To add salt to the wounds, Marsh ended up with Huckins' boat. When a fire destroyed Marsh's sawmill at Marsh's Falls (circa 1892), Marsh made Huntsville his navigation headquarters. Here he locked horns with another steamboating giant, Captain Denton, and ended up controlling the Huntsville and Lake of Bays Transportation Company in 1895.

9   BIRKENDALE ROCK CUT

Continuing south on Highway 35, you come to Birkendale, where William Grieves Robson and his family settled in 1883. The Robsons operated a post office and a tourist home named Birkendale. The Birks and Dales were pioneers here, although it is not entirely clear if that is the reason behind the name of the community.

There are two rock cuts just south of Birkendale. The first is a typical Muskoka rock cut, but the second is very dramatic. In the east face of the cut, there's a recumbent fold accentuated by a broad black band that bends back on itself like a loop of licorice. Geologists describe the rocks as gently inclined gneiss and granulite.

The Muskoka section of the Canadian Shield is referred to as the Central Gneiss Belt, a very complex terrain. Gneiss is a metamorphic rock composed of quartz, feldspar and mica, and is distinguished by its banded, or layered, structure. These rocks were once deep within the earth's crust, where excessive heat allowed them to flow like toothpaste squeezed from a tube. Most of the patterns you see in the rocks today were created in this way,

As you drive towards Dorset, you'll notice the landscape has closed in on you, as if you were trekking through a mountain pass. The road slips by tall, threatening hills and pleasant valleys with tantalizing, but brief, glimpses of Lake of Bays.

10   DORSET LOOKOUT TOWER

Watch for the lookout tower turnoff on the right as you drive south. The road to the top is steep, but well maintained. At the base of the lookout tower there's a park area with spectacular views of its own. But if you want the very best views, views that will take your breath away, then you must ascend the metal superstructure and ignore the ghostly whine of the wind, and the creaks and groans of the staircase. If your bravery has caught up with you at the midway point, you'll push on to the top and feel very accomplished as you survey the countryside. On a sunny autumn day the hills are a quilt of colour surrounding ruffled blue lakes.

If you're congratulating yourself for reaching the top, consider the fire rangers who manned the previous lookout, which was built in 1922. The only way up in those days was an iron ladder with guide rings. The original tower was replaced in 1967. The observation deck is 142 metres above lake level and provides a view of 803 square kilometres.

11   JOHNNYCAKE BAY

There's a north and south entrance to Dorset. If you bypass the first turnoff and continue over the Highway 35 bridge, you'll see Trading (or Johnnycake) Bay on the left before turning into Dorset.

Lake of Bays was called Trading Lake, owing to the evidence of trading posts discovered by Alexander Shirreff on his 1829 expedition. The name Johnnycake Bay traces its roots to the days of the Shrigley mill on the Hollow River (which flows into the bay from Kawagama Lake). The Shrigleys built a sawmill and a grist mill in 1874. Those first summers yielded good crops of corn, which they ground at their mill. The abundance of cornmeal, coupled with a series of mild winters during which maple syrup could be made, gave rise to the consumption of huge amounts of johnnycake and maple syrup — hence the name Johnnycake Bay.

12   DORSET

Dorset is a little town with big intentions. It is unabashedly entrepreneurial, with gift shops, ice cream bars, and general stores all crowding for front-line positions along the main street. It's a town that has grown like topsy, always bustling with people and backed up with cars. The attraction? Well, Robinson's General Store for one. Voted Canada's best country store, it draws people like the Food Building at the Toronto Exhibition. Inside, you can buy anything from a mackinaw jacket to a sink faucet. It's a grocery store, service station, gift store, eatery and hardware store all in one.

It's appropriate that this store sits on the site of Zac Cole's first hotel. Zac Cole was the founder of the community. He arrived in 1862, having earlier left the Boshkung Narrows area (Haliburton) for a period of time to serve as a soldier in the American Civil War. From all accounts he was one of those rough-edged "movers and shakers" who didn't mind a good drink now and again. He told his wife that when he died he wanted to be buried in a tamarack coffin — one that snapped loudly when it burned. He said he knew he was going to hell, so he might as well let them know he'd arrived.

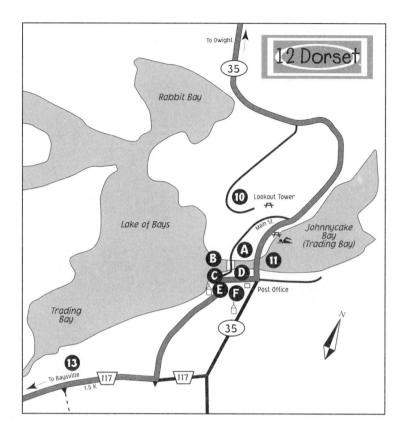

Dorset was first called Cedar Narrows for the cedar trees along the narrows. Zac Cole changed the name to Colebridge when he surveyed the town in 1879. When applying for a post office in 1883, he found that a Colebridge already existed. The name Dorset was chosen instead, probably because an early surveyor, Thomas Ridout, came from Dorsetshire, England.

Dorset is cut in two by a county line that runs down the main street. The Lake of Bays side of town is in Muskoka, and the east side in Haliburton. (Robinson's Store is in Haliburton, Clayton's in Muskoka.)

12A ROBINSON'S GENERAL STORE

Zachariah Cole's Colebridge Hotel was situated where Robinson's General Store is today. Cole ventured into the area as a surveyor when he helped cut the line of the Bobcaygeon Road. He returned in 1862 with his family and built the Colebridge, the first hotel in Dorset. It burned soon after Cole's death in 1885 and was replaced by the Fairview (it also burned). The Red Onion Hotel replaced it. Fred McKey purchased the property and built a store, which mushroomed into the present Robinson's General Store.

Robinson's General Store.
PHOTO COURTESY BRAD ROBINSON

Harry Robinson married Fred McKey's widow Marguerite. They lived for a time in the old Red Onion hotel, them moved above the store. It wasn't until after the Second World War that they changed the name to Robinson's. At that time, the fur trade was brisk. Traders brought their pelts into Robinson's for sale to the Hudson's Bay Company. "I remember the floor piled up with beaver skins three feet deep," Brad Robinson says. He's been operating the store since 1955. In 1981 Robinson's was voted "Canada's Best Country Store, in *Today* magazine.

12B THE NARROWS

The construction of the dam at Baysville raised water levels on Lake of Bays. Prior to that the narrows at Dorset were so shallow that a horse and wagon could ford the stream without difficulty. When the Bobcaygeon Road pushed through in 1859, workmen built a wooden bridge. In 1914 the Western Bridge and Equipment Company of Chatham erected an arched steel bridge which has seen further improvements over the years.

12C CLAYTON'S GENERAL STORE (now Trading Bay Marina)

Clayton's General Store dates to 1907, when a previous owner, Newton Langford, rebuilt after a fire. The building also served as the post office — depending on the politics of the day. Newton Langford lost the postal contract when the Liberals came into power, but Ed Speers, who succeeded Langford as store owner in 1912, brought the post office back to this location when the

View of Dorset, looking north. The Dorset Hotel and Burk and Avery's store are seen on the right. PHOTO COURTESY BRAD ROBINSON

Conservatives reclaimed office. Wes Clayton took over the store and the post-master's job in 1922, passing on the store and the post master's job to his son Jack, who died in October 1994. Many people remember the Claytons' hospitality. They had the first television in Dorset and their store became a meeting place, particularly on Saturday night when the hockey crowd arrived to watch the game.

12D DORSET HOTEL SITE

Across the street from Clayton's, the Dorset Hotel and Burk and Avery's store dominated the scene in the early days. Dorset Hotel started out as an unpretentious little boarding house, but grew into the largest hotel in Dorset, a red brick building encircled with balconies. It was known by various names over the years: the McIlroy, the Iroquois, the Narrows, the Dorset House and the Lumberjack Inn. Today it's The Fiery Grill restaurant. A parking lot has usurped the place of Burk and Avery's store, which burned in 1944. The Fiery Grill restaurant pays tribute to the lumbering heritage of the village. The walls are lined with dozens of old photographs and logging artifacts.

12E THE ALVIRA HOTEL (Rumours Restaurant)

Across the street from the Iroquois Hotel, Newton Langford built a sizable resort, which he named after his wife, Eunice Alvira Langford. The hotel stayed in business from 1904 to 1927. When it burned that year, it was called the Ganoseyo ("good house").

12F KNOX UNITED CHURCH

Built in 1894, Knox United started out as a Presbyterian church on land donated by Angus MacKay and Frances Harvie (also spelled Harvey). MacKay had built a sawmill in Dorset that year. He donated the first lumber he cut at the mill for the construction of the church. Parishioners in Dorset were among the first to recognize that it seemed excessive to have both a Presbyterian and Methodist minister in one small town. They actually united several years before the Methodists and Presbyterians officially amalgamated in 1925. That same year, the residents built a stone wall around the church to keep the cows out. In the church's centennial year, 1994, the wall was rebuilt and dedicated to Norman MacKay, a lifelong member of the church and the son of Angus MacKay.

At one time in the church's history, the only person who could play the organ was a young girl whose feet could not reach the pedals. Other youngsters took turns crouching under the organ stool and pumping the organ pedals with their hands.

Main Street leaves the village via Pill Hill, named for the drug store that used to be situated downhill from St. Mary Magdelene Anglican Church. The road intersects with Muskoka Road 118 West. Turn right and continue along the road.

13 GILMOUR TRAMWAY LOCATION (4950 Muskoka Road 117)

Watch for the hydro transformer on the left, precisely one and a half kilometres from the Dorset turnoff. Near this spot, the famous Gilmour tramway traversed what is now Muskoka Road 117 on its way from Lake of Bays to the height of land on the south side of the road.

David Gilmour created the ingenious device to move logs *uphill* from the Muskoka River watershed to the Trent River watershed, and on to his mill in Trenton. The tramway consisted of a series of jackladders and a log slide that moved the logs about two kilometres inland, to a height of 36 metres. At the top of the rise, the logs tumbled into the waterway and were driven down to St. Nora Lake, and on to Trenton. The logs entered St. Nora Lake where the Leslie M. Frost Natural Resources Centre is today.

Work on the tramway began in 1893 and the first drive started in 1894. Unfortunately it took two years to get the logs to the mill so the project was abandoned. You can see pictures of the tramway at Robinson's General Store, in Dorset. On the shore of Lake of Bays, the tramway powerhouse has been converted into a pretty stone cottage.

Gilmour Tramway. NAC C21225

14   DORSET RESEARCH CENTRE
(Bellwood Acres Road)

The Dorset Research Centre is recognized around the world for its research on acid rain, mercury contamination and nutrient levels in lakes. A division of the provincial Ministry of Energy and Environment, the Dorset Research Centre began life in a trailer near Vankoughnet in 1975. It moved to this site in 1980. Research at this centre determined that the acid rain affecting Muskoka's lakes was predominantly a result of industry in the Ohio Valley. With this evidence, Canada was able to lobby the United States to reduce its sulphur emissions (the cause of acid rain) by 10 million tons per annum by the year 2000.

Continue along Muskoka Road 117 until you reach the turnoff for the old highway, which takes you along the shores of Lakes of Bays.

15   LAKE OF BAYS PARK

The Lake of Bays Park, just east of the Bigwin wharf, is a welcome addition to this stretch of roadway. Purchased by Lake of Bays Township in 1986, the park has an excellent boat-launching facility and dock, as well as a swimming beach.

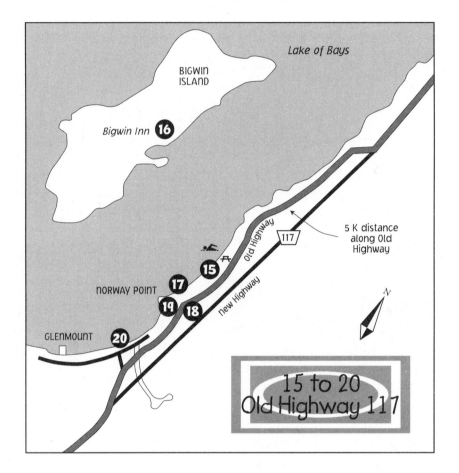

The sun-rippled shallows invite you to roll up your trousers and wade far out into the bay. But don't let the gentle shorelines fool you. At its deepest point, Lake of Bays plunges 79 metres (260 feet).

Lurking in those depths is the fabled Lake of Bays monster, which is supposed to resemble a giant sturgeon. People have seen it frisking about in the Bigwin Island area. There are some who believe it could be a relic of prehistoric days, a fish that just grew and grew.

16 BIGWIN ISLAND AND BIGWIN INN

Nothing stirs the heart like the sight of the late, great Bigwin Inn, crumbling away on the shore of Bigwin Island. You can just see it from the mainland, where Old Highway 117 dips close to Lake of Bays. When you cruise close to the island in a boat, you can see that the sides of building are falling away like paint off a peeling deck chair. Even after years of neglect, the dining room and dance pavilion of the world-famous inn are still impressive.

Aerial view of the Bigwin Inn
showing (from left to right) the dining room, waterfront and dance hall.

Charles Orlando Shaw, the visionary who dreamed up the resort, was a major shareholder in the Huntsville, Lake of Bays Navigation Company when he bought Bigwin Island in 1911. Someone had suggested the navigation company's business would improve if there was an island hotel accessed only by boat. Others say Shaw had tried to get a room at the WaWa Hotel, across the lake, and couldn't, so he vowed to build a bigger, better hotel of his own.

Even now, in faded glory, the place stirs a romantic vision of ladies in fine dresses floating over ballroom floors or being helped into mahogany launches for a whirl around the lake. The place fairly dripped money — so much so that you could excuse people for their slip of the tongue in calling it the Big*wig* Inn. Clark Gable and Carol Lombard stayed here, as did the Rockefellers and the Wrigleys.

The inn takes its name from the island, which belonged at one time to Chief John Bigwin. The Bigwin family claimed this part of Muskoka as their hunting ground. Bigwin and other chiefs relinquished the land in treaties during the 1830s-1850s. The Bigwin family moved to Rama, but Chief Bigwin continued to summer in this part of Muskoka.

Since fire was a constant threat to the early resorts, Shaw decided to build his hotel of fireproof stone and concrete. Shortly after he bought the island, Shaw employed architect John Wilson to draw up plans for Bigwin Inn, but the inn did not open until 1920, owing to slow progress during World War One.

At its zenith the hotel was one of the best in North America, entertaining royalty and top-ranking government officials. The grounds were impeccably groomed and crisscrossed by covered walkways. Ties and tails were a must in the dining room, where the lilting airs of chamber music accentuated the hushed atmosphere. Everything was tasteful and dignified, even the recreational pursuits: tennis, golf, lawn bowling, croquet.

The one thing Shaw would not tolerate was alcohol. The Bigwin Inn was totally dry under Shaw's tenure (at least in the public areas.)

After C.O. Shaw died in 1942, the resort passed through several owners and declined. A new condominium project breathed some life back into the island. The remainder of the resort and the island itself is now owned by Alan Peters, who plans to establish a golf course and recreational community.

17 BIGWIN WHARF

Adjacent to the Lake of Bays Park are the Bigwin Inn parking area and riding stables. There were once five or six stable buildings flanking the green one, which is still standing. Bigwin guests parked here and waited at the wharf for the Bigwin steamer to ferry them across to the island.

18 WAWA SPRING HOUSE (Robertson Family Historic Marker)

Across from the Bigwin Island Resort Condominium driveway is a marker erected by the ruins of the WaWa "spring house." The spring house was a shady retreat built around a natural spring. The Robertson family erected the plaque in memory of George and Elizabeth Robertson, the first settlers on Norway Point. The Robertsons came to the area 1873. In 1896 they started taking summer guests in their farmhouse. Later they sold the land to the Canadian Railway News Company, which erected the ill-fated WaWa Hotel in 1907. The hotel opened the following year.

19 WAWA HOTEL SITE

The WaWa, which means "wild goose," came to a tragic end on an August evening in 1923 when a fire ripped through it, killing 11 people. The fire lit up the sky for miles, and people as far away as Baysville said the light was so bright you could pick up a pin in the street. The resort was situated adjacent to the Bigwin wharf. In its day the WaWa was a grand and prestigious hotel with many modern innovations, including a searchlight, which the brochure described as "a novel and interesting feature new to Canada and very popular in resorts in Switzerland." The brochure promised a healthful respite from the city — and no mosquitoes!

Although the resort had one of the finest spots for a hotel site, the WaWa was never rebuilt after the fire.

The WaWa waterfront stretched from the tip of Norway Point along a beautiful beach. You can see the exact location when you're standing on the Norway Point Church dock (see below). While still impressive, the beach is a sliver of its former self, as the construction of the Baysville dam raised water levels and drowned several feet of the sandy shore.

20 SIDE TRIP NORWAY POINT AND GLENMOUNT
(Distance: 2.5 kilometres)

Turn right at Glenmount Road to visit the community of Norway Point. The road runs towards the water, then forks right and left. The right branch takes you to the picturesque Norway Point Church, while the left road hugs the shoreline and continues to the sailing club wharf.

Among Norway Point's prominent settlers were Scottish immigrants who arrived around the year 1875. They liked the area because it reminded them of home. However, they soon discovered the land was stony and unproductive. Many gave up their land claims and vacated.

Prior to the turn of the century, Rev. J.L. Brown held one of his first church services under a huge tree in his grove. He was able to raise enough money to construct the Norway Point church in 1908. The church collapsed under the weight of Muskoka's snows and was replaced in July of 1944.

Also at the turn of the century, the citizens of Norway Point laid out a private golf course behind what is presently the Glenmount Dock. The group of 10 paid approximately $50 each for the section of land, a sum that allowed them exclusive use of the nine-hole course. Though overgrown today, the recreational facility was once a source of great amusement to vacationers of both the WaWa and Glenmount hotels.

The Glenmount Hotel sat where the tennis courts are, behind the sailing clubhouse. The clubhouse used to be the Roman Catholic Church. Next to it was the Glenmount post office and a general store. The Glenmount Hotel, like the WaWa, is now just a picture on a faded postcard, a memory of another era.

Backtracking to Muskoka Road 117 and continuing to Baysville brings the circle tour to its conclusion.

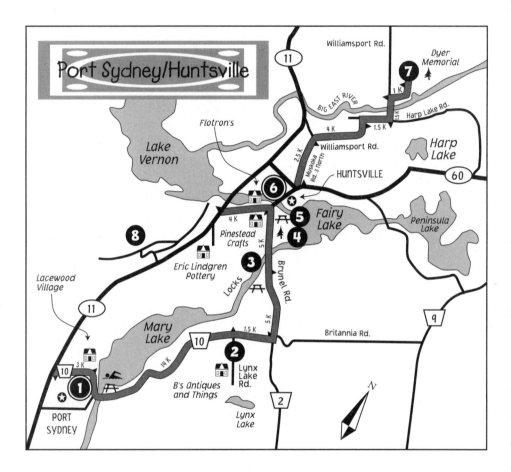

Port Sydney/Huntsville

Williamsport Rd.

11

Dyer Memorial

7

1 K

BIG EAST RIVER

.5 K

Harp Lake Rd.

4 K

1.5 K

Williamsport Rd.

Harp Lake

Flotron's

Lake Vernon

2.5 K

HUNTSVILLE

60

6

Fairy Lake

5

4

Peninsula Lake

4 K

8

Pinestead Crafts

5 K

3

Brunel Rd.

Eric Lindgren Pottery

Lacewood Village

11

Locks

Mary Lake

10

1.5 K

5 K

Britannia Rd.

9

14 K

2

Lynx Lake Rd.

3 K

B's Antiques and Things

N

10

1

Lynx Lake

2

PORT SYDNEY

CHAPTER 7

Port Sydney/Huntsville

Distance: 27 kilometres (17 miles)

T he Port Sydney/Huntsville tour is a favourite of mine. It's a short, scenic trip that encompasses the small-village charm of Port Sydney and the big-town amenities of Huntsville. The Muskoka Pioneer Village, in Huntsville, is perhaps the best attraction in Muskoka. The village brings the past to life. It's expertly done and lots of fun for old and young alike.

Commencing at the intersection of Highway 11 North and Muskoka Road 10, this route takes you through Port Sydney, with a stop at the falls, and continues around Mary Lake to the Brunel Locks.

After travelling through Huntsville, there are two optional side trips, north to the Dyer Memorial or south to Madill Church. The Dyer Memorial is a bit out of the way, but well worth every kilometre. This diamond-in-the-rough park is awesome in itself, but getting there, over tortuous terrain, is half the fun.

— Attractions —

Muskoka Pioneer Village
Brunel Road
Huntsville
705-789-7576

— Antiques —

B's Antiques and Things
Lynx Lake Road
 (off Muskoka Road 10)
705-789-7929

— Sights —

Port Sydney Beach
Indian Landing
Scenic Falls and
  Port Sydney Dam
Brunel Locks
Lookout Mountain
Madill Church
Dyer Memorial

— Arts and Crafts —

Lacewood Village
Muskoka Road 10
Port Sydney
705-385-0717

Flotron's Huntsville Trading Co
18 Main Street
Huntsville
705-789-4220

Pinestead Crafts
Brunel Road
Huntsville
705-789-1171

Lindgren Pottery
Lindgren Road (Off Highway 11)
705-789-2843

1   PORT SYDNEY

The sign at the entrance of this town says: "Welcome to Port Sydney, the home of 500 nice people and one old grouch!" I have yet to find the grouch. Besides, who could be grouchy in Port Sydney? At one end of town, you've got the lake on your doorstep; at the other, a cascade of water that slides over the rocks like honey.

Early travel writers remarked that Port Sydney resembled an English seaside village. Elements of the British personality remain. The beach area is as festive as the seaside in the summer, and one old homestead sports the traditional dry-stone retaining walls so popular in the British isles.

In its early years Port Sydney embodied the British attitudes of its founder, Albert Sydney-Smith. Sydney-Smith was a man of independent means who enjoyed playing the role of a benevolent country squire. He visited the area in

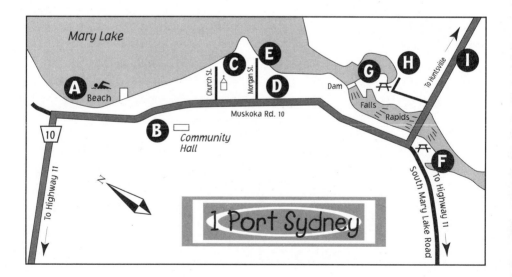

John MacAlpine's sawmill by the falls at Port Sydney. PHOTO COURTESY OF GEORGE JOHNSON

1871 and, finding the land to his liking, acquired the lots abandoned by the first settler, John McAlpine.

McAlpine had been in the area since 1868, often providing the dubious service of transporting settlers to their locations — down the rapids in a dugout canoe called the Man-Killer.

McAlpine built a sawmill at the outlet of Mary Lake. Sydney-Smith acquired this when he took over McAlpine's land. At that time most of the settlers had congregated farther north (near the present town dock). Sydney-Smith felt a good village should revolve around its mill, so he subdivided his land and created a community. He registered the plans in 1873. Those men who had helped with the project had streets named after them: William Morgan, Isaac Fawcett and Robert Goodwin. In 1874 the plan was extended to include settlement at the north end of town, and the Mary Lake Post Office was renamed Port Sydney, in honour of its founder.

Sydney-Smith donated land for a church, and added a grist and oatmeal mill to his sawmill operations. He was, in every sense, the benefactor of the town, enjoying the respect accorded his position, while at the same time providing social and civic amenities that strengthened the community.

With the opening of the locks on the Muskoka River in 1875, Port Sydney rose to prominence as a major distribution centre. Steamboats carried goods and passengers to Huntsville and Hoodstown. But what the locks gave the community, the railway took away. In spite of the pleas of the townspeople, the railway bypassed the community on its route north. Port Sydney became a backwater — but a beautiful one. That beauty, unmarred by freight yards or industrial development, gave Port Sydney the edge as a tourist retreat. It is still one of the prettiest spots in Muskoka.

1A   PORT SYDNEY BEACH

The beach faces three islands. The closest one, in direct line with the dock, is a monolithic clump of stone appropriately called Rocky Island. The smooth curve of the central island gave the lake its Indian name, Kche-negeek-chiching ("the Place of the Great Otter"), because it resembled a diving otter. Today it is called Crown Island after Edward Crown, who purchased land in Port Sydney in 1879.

Alexander Murray explored this area for the Geological Survey of Canada in 1853. He named the lake after his daughter, Mary.

1B   H.R. BROWN HOUSE (1886)

This charming stone house has been in the Brown family for generations. Hugh R. Brown moved into the house in 1894. He came to Port Sydney hoping to farm, as most settlers did, but turned to the lumber business when confronted with the rocky Muskoka landscape. Brown changed the roof line of the house and added the verandah in 1903.

The house was built for Eloisa Girdlestone way back in 1886. The builder made the rough-hewn stones of this building look like ashlar (squared stone) by etching the mortar when it was wet. The dry-stone retaining wall, constructed in 1920, is an interesting feature reminiscent of those in the British isles.

Doug and Marylysbeth Brown own the home today. H.R. Brown was Doug's grandfather.

IC   CHRIST CHURCH

(at the foot of Christ Church Street overlooking Mary Lake)

Built in 1873, Christ Church is the oldest surviving Anglican church in Muskoka. Albert Sydney-Smith donated this picturesque piece of land and cut the lumber for the church in his mill. The local residents hand-planed the boards before putting them in place. The lych-gate was originally designed as a place where pallbearers could set down a coffin while waiting for the clergyman to arrive. Today it bears a plaque in memory of Albert Sydney-Smith, the founder of the village.

1D WHAT'S COOKING (Foundations of Sydney Hotel)

What's Cooking is the restaurant built on the foundation of the Sydney Hotel, erected in the early 1870s by a Welshman named William H. Morgan. Morgan helped Albert Sydney-Smith with his plans to create a village and had a street named after him. Morgan was responsible for the fine woodwork inside Christ Church.

1E THE CHEESE FACTORY

The Port Sydney Cheese Factory was built by the entrance to the river in 1897. The steamer *Gem* (often called the milk boat) made trips around the lake collecting milk for the factory. Factory hands disposed of the waste products of the operation in an ingenious manner. They pumped the whey via a submarine line to the opposite side of the river, which was home for a robust group of swine. The pigs disposed of the whey in a most efficient manner, but were poorly rewarded for their efforts — as you can well imagine.

IF INDIAN LANDING

The gravel bar on the southwest side of the bridge has come to be known as Indian Landing. In fact, the Indian portage route actually followed the east bank of the river and the name is incorrect, although pretty and entirely suitable. At this point the waters of the north branch of the Muskoka River flow in shallow riffles over sunlit gravel. In *Port Sydney Past*, George Johnson says, "In recent years, bulldozers have been used to clear a channel and reduce the rapids to a pitiful travesty of what they once were." The rapids caused problems for the lumbermen, who built a shallow dam on the river here to "drown" the rapids during the spring log drive.

IG SCENIC DAM AND MILL SITE

The Port Sydney falls do not froth and churn like others in Muskoka. The water flows fast and smooth — like liquid glass. Very pretty. The rocks at the falls' edge were once an island, with water flowing on both sides. This is the site of both the McAlpine and Sydney-Smith sawmills. When Albert Sydney-Smith acquired McAlpine's Mill, he enlarged it and added a grist mill. He marketed the flour from this mill under the name "Staff of Life." The sawmill cut about 10,000 board feet of lumber each day.

The area around the two mills was built up to a height of ten feet using wooden retaining walls and sawdust. The sawdust eroded away after the mills were demolished in 1930, leaving the bare rocks as they were in John McAlpine's day.

IH CONSTRUCTION OF STEAMER *Northern* (Historic Marker)

Just up the road from the dam, a plaque marks the place where Denton, Smiley and Company built the steamer *Northern* in 1877. The side-wheeler was the first steamboat to ply on the Mary-Fairy-Vernon lake chain. The boat would have been restricted to Mary Lake were it not for a government project to install locks on the Muskoka River (1875). The locks removed the waterfall that had blocked navigation between Fairy and Mary lakes.

The steamboat service to Huntsville and Hoodstown was a boon to Port Sydney. Passengers bound for the northern sections of Muskoka preferred the waterways to the roadways; as such, all traffic flowed through the town at the foot of the lake system — in this case, Port Sydney.

Denton added more steamboats to his fleet and moved his base of operations to Huntsville. His company was later taken over by Captain Marsh, who formed the Huntsville and Lake of Bays Transportation Company in 1895.

1-I MUSKOKA ROAD 10/BRUNEL ROAD

At this point the tour leaves Port Sydney and continues along Muskoka Road 10, originally called the Brunel Road.

In 1868 surveyor Walter Beatty laid out a road that led east from the Muskoka Colonization Road, along the Sixth Concession Line of Stephenson Township, around Mary Lake, to the eastern boundary of Brunel Township. Beatty had many such roads to locate and pushed this one through in record time. Port Sydney historian George Johnson says, "He spent only two weeks doing work in Stephenson and Brunel, and the road builders spent the next hundred years making changes in his route." In many cases, he chose the steepest right of way, when there were less tortuous passages through the countryside.

Today the route is beautiful because of the hills, and I would not want to be rid of a single one of them.

2 GHOST TOWNS

Blink and you'd miss what used to be a pioneer community at the Lynx Lake turnoff. The northerly extension of that roadway is completely overgrown with mature trees. At this crossroads was the community of Seely, named for the Seely family, whose property bounded the four corners. There was a post office here and a school. The school, situated on the southwest corner of the intersection, was later converted into a home.

Another pioneer community, called Candytown, has disappeared into the bush as well, although the name survives in on a road sign.

At the intersection of Muskoka Road 10 and Brunel Road, turn left towards Huntsville.

3   BRUNEL LOCK (site of Fetterly and Cottrill Sawmill)
The construction of the lock removed the only drawback to navigation on the Mary-Fairy-Vernon lake chain: a ten-foot waterfall and rapids at the foot of Fairy Lake. The lock was ready for use in 1875, but shoals had to be dredged out of the river before navigation between Fairy and Mary lakes could begin.

At the upper end of the lock chamber, you'll notice a small swing bridge. Although there's no reason for it today, it once gave access to the longest operating water-powered sawmill in Muskoka. The building sat on the east side of the dam.

John Fetterly built the sawmill in 1873. Later he added a grist mill. After changing hands several times, the mill was acquired by the Cottrill family, who continued sawing lumber until 1954.

The Brunel Lock on the Muskoka River.
The wooden swing bridge is in the closed position
giving access to the Cottrill sawmill.
PHOTO COURTESY OF GEORGE JOHNSON

The Brunel Locks, Huntsville.
PHOTO BY G.W. CAMPBELL

"All the timber from Mary Lake was, of necessity, brought through the locks on 60-foot rafts. We had one colourful character, Bill Hutchins, who could not swim. It was a habit of men working on the logs to frequently have one or two boom chains over their shoulders. Bill Hutchins was seen to fall off one of these rafts into about 10 feet of water with two boom chains around his neck. Everyone came to his rescue, but it was found that he was standing on the shore of the channel. He later stated that he could not swim and had simply walked across the river bottom and up the other side. If you will visit the locks around 5 o'clock on a quiet June morning and look at the bottom above the old Locks Bridge, you can see the tracks where Bill walked across the river bottom some 50 odd years ago."

Frank Hutcheson
From the Muskoka History lecture series, 1974

4   MUSKOKA PIONEER VILLAGE

The hustle and bustle of a crossroads community comes alive at Muskoka Pioneer Village — it's almost like stepping into a scene from the television series, Road to Avonlea. Inside the Spence Inn, a museum interpreter, in her role as innkeeper, invites you to choose the room you'd like. "But if you decide to stay," she says, "remember we tolerate no liquor on the premises." Meanwhile the robust cook, with flour up to her elbows, winks at you as she kneads the dough and promises she can fetch you "a wee drop, in secret" if you'd like it. Farther up the street, a smithy pummels a horseshoe into shape at his forge. In the dim interiors of a spartan log home, a pioneer homemaker bundles fresh herbs and ties them to the rafters, while her friend spins wool by the window.

Fourteen restored buildings, collected from various locations in the district, represent a typical pioneer community in the years from 1860 to 1910. You can take a horse-drawn wagon ride around the property, taste pioneer cooking, or hike along the Cann Lake Trail. The village hosts some unique events throughout the year, including the pioneer logging games, the pig-calling contest, and an annual Victorian Christmas.

The village is one of the best attractions in Muskoka. Go. You'll love it.

Muskoka Pioneer Village, Huntsville. PHOTO BY G.W. CAMPBELL

5   LOOKOUT MOUNTAIN (Lions Lookout)

Well, it's not really a mountain, but it's been called that for so long, who's going to argue. Certainly not me. The road up to the Lions Lookout is definitely mountain-like. To avoid accidents, there's an "up" route and a "down" route.

At the top you get an excellent view of Fairy Lake. Alexander Murray named the lake for its beauty on a surveying trip in 1853. At the foot of Lookout Mountain, Alexander Bailey opened a trading post. Here he exchanged clothing and food for furs from the Indians. Bailey also operated a similar store on the Muskoka River near Bracebridge and built that town's first sawmill and grist mill. This man covered considerable area, having an impact on the earliest history of Bracebridge, Huntsville and Port Carling, where he eventually settled. Part French and part Indian, he fit our grade-school description of a *coureur de bois*, a "runner of the woods."

After the Muskoka area was opened for settlement, the Indians moved farther north to get their furs. Bailey abandoned the post. For many years a rotting wharf and the remains of a boat were visible at the bottom of the lake at Lookout Mountain and thought to be remnants of those trading-post days.

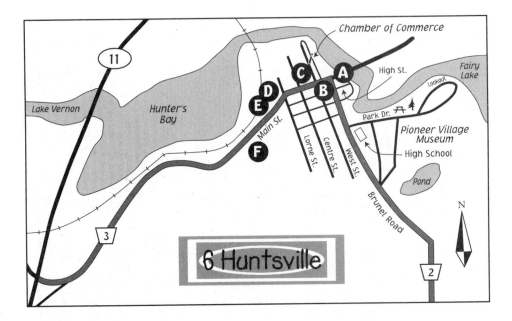

6   HUNTSVILLE

Huntsville is named after its first permanent settler, Captain George Hunt. Hunt settled on the east side of the Muskoka River in 1869 and set about organizing the first school, the first church services (held in his home) and the first retail store.

When he arrived the Muskoka Road had not yet reached Lake Vernon, but by 1870, through Hunt's efforts, new settlers had proper road access and a post office — named Huntsville in his honour.

Later Hunt subdivided his land and sold lots to abstainers. As an ardent temperance man, Hunt incorporated a "no drinking" clause into his deeds, effective throughout his lifetime. This accounts for the development of the town on the west side of the river, where there are difficult hills, rather than on the flat east side, where his restrictions applied.

The construction of locks on the Muskoka River provided an impetus for growth by opening navigation on the Mary-Fairy-Vernon lake chain in 1875. Huntsville became a port of call for the steamer *Northern*.

Meanwhile a rival community had evolved on the opposite shores of Lake Vernon. Hoodstown, founded by Captain Charles Hood, showed every promise of becoming a distribution centre. At one point it looked like the railway might run through the community. Huntsville's town fathers, however, convinced the rail authorities that Huntsville would make the better lumbering centre.

Main Street Huntsville, looking east. The town hall is visible in the centre of the photograph. The clock in the tower came from Union Station. PHOTO COURTESY OF BERYL MUNRO

The railway arrived in Huntsville in 1886, promising a bright future for Huntsville, but tolling a death knell for Hoodstown. Huntsville achieved village status immediately, Hoodstown faded away. Little trace of it remains today.

Without a backward look at its fallen competitor, Huntsville raced on. Stores and hotels sprang up. Lumber companies latched onto the shorelines of Hunter's Bay.

On April 18, 1894 the town suffered its first major setback, a fire destroyed most of the businesses on the main street. Hoping to save their stock, the clerks from the Hutcheson General Store loaded goods onto the steamer *Excelsior*, but an oil leak from another store had trickled onto the river and ignited. The *Excelsior* drifted into the swirling flames and caught fire. The store owners lost everything.

The businessmen rallied and rebuilt, passing a bylaw permitting only brick, iron or stone buildings to be constructed in the village core. Today Huntsville is the largest town in Muskoka — a fact that can be attributed to the excellent year-round vacation opportunities on nearby Fairy and Peninsula lakes — the mecca for cross-country ski enthusiasts and Muskoka's downhill ski centre, Hidden Valley.

6A ALL SAINTS' ANGLICAN CHURCH

It's worth straying from the Brunel Road/Main Street route to see All Saints' Church, one of Huntsville's striking architectural features. As you enter the town, turn right at High Street and park at the parish hall.

When Captain Hunt arrived in Huntsville he found trapper William Cann's log shanty on the slope of land near the river. Cann donated this land to the Church of England in 1876. By this time he had established himself as a hotelkeeper in the pioneer community.

Cann left the town some years later because of financial difficulties. Still, you can't help but remember him when you see what's become of his gift to the town.

With land of their own at last, the Anglican congregation hastily erected a church hall, which served as a place of worship until 1895. At that time they moved into their beautiful stone church, which had been under construction since 1889. The original meeting hall burned in the great fire of 1894.

As a pioneer church, All Saints' stands out as a project of cathedral-like ambition. Outside it resembles a medieval castle. Inside the vaulted ceiling resounds with the richness and warmth of polished wood. At the base of the arches there are tall, thin windows in stained glass, each one a work of art. The driving force behind the church project and its companion, the parish hall (also of stone), was Rev. Thomas Llwyd, who served as Anglican priest from 1883 to 1903.

6B TOWN HALL

Built in 1926 the town hall also housed the jail, courthouse, armouries, post office and auditorium. The tower clock came from the old Union Station in Toronto. Mr. Briggs, a Huntsville jeweller, supervised the transportation and installation of the clock in its new location. Since the tower in Huntsville was smaller than the tower at Union Station, Briggs had to fashion new dials, hands and connections for the clock, using pieces from old car parts.

6C SITE OF ALLAN SHAY'S LOG HOME

The northeast corner of Main Street and Centre Street (Becker's location) marks the site of Allan Shay's two-storey log home. When Shay built it in the late 1860s, it was the first substantial house in the area. Shay owned 100 acres of land on this side of the river. When he subdivided his holdings into town lots, he named the streets after members of his family: Duncan, Cora, Florence, Lorne and Minerva.

In later years workmen dismantled Shay's home, log by log, marking each one. They hoped to reconstruct the home as a memorial, but the logs rotted in storage in the tannery yard without anyone taking charge of the project.

All Saints' Anglican Church, Huntsville. PHOTO BY G.W. CAMPBELL

6D WILGRESS BUILDING (Muskoka Wood Company)

Built as a residence by Huntsville lawyer George Wilgress in the 1890s, this pretty grey brick building was once the corporate headquarters of the legendary Muskoka Wood Manufacturing Company.

In 1902 Mr. R.J. Hutcheson purchased the Whaley Lumber Company on Hunter's Bay and announced his intention of cutting hardwood. It was a revolutionary idea at the time. Muskoka's hardwood had been ignored because it sank when loggers attempted to float it downriver to the mills. The softwood lumber companies scoffed at Hutcheson's idea and gave him about three years to survive. Hutcheson found that if he peeled the bark from the hardwood trees and left them to dry for two or three weeks, they could "float all summer if necessary".

The Muskoka Wood Company was the first integrated hardwood mill in Canada. Hutcheson's detractors ate their words when the softwood supplies dwindled and the hardwood industry supported the town. Muskoka Wood's Red Deer brand of hardwood flooring received worldwide acclaim. The mill also produced handles for brushes and brooms, chair parts and dowels. The original mill burned in 1922 and was rebuilt.

6E BAYVIEW HOTEL (Vernon House)

The Cook family moved to Huntsville in 1890. They built the Vernon House on land they acquired from pioneer settler James Hanes. The hotel had a pleasant aspect overlooking Lake Vernon and was within walking distance of the railway station. At that time it catered to the affluent society, setting the scene for elegant afternoon teas and soirees. Given the hotel's upper-crust background, it is a sad twist of fate to discover that the porter who met the trains could not pronounce the name correctly and called out, "Anyone for Vermin House?"

In the 1920s the Muskoka Wood Company bought the hotel and used it mainly as a boarding house for their workers. At this time the name changed to the Bayview Hotel. Today it is the home of Chumly's Tap and Grill.

6F PAGET HOUSE

A landmark in Huntsville since 1903, the Paget House is a rare architectural treat. The twin turrets give the house a mansion-like appearance. Indeed, its owner, George Paget, was one of Huntsville's leading citizens, a man who could well afford a home of this distinction. Already a successful grain merchant, he moved to Huntsville in 1879 and established himself in the lumber business. He sat on the first town council in 1901 and was the assessment commissioner. His son Arthur, who inherited the house, was also active in politics and served as mayor of Huntsville in 1919 and 1920. He and his brother, Charles, patented a grain door invention in 1923, setting up three cooper yards in Buffalo to make the device.

The house sat empty in a shroud of scruffy spruce trees for many years, until local contractor Larry French decided to restore the home to its former grandeur. The Frenchs held a grand opening for the project in the summer of 1990. It is now being used as an office building.

The road continues out of town and joins Highway 11 at the overpass. At this point the tour ends, but you may wish to visit two other sites in the area: the Dyer Memorial Park, located about 11 kilometres (seven miles) north of Huntsville, and the Madill Church, a few kilometres to the south.

7 DYER MEMORIAL

(Starting at the corner of Highway 60 and Muskoka Road 3 North, continue past the Huntsville Hospital. Turn right at Williamsport Road and watch for the signs. Distance: 11 kilometres.)

Dyer Memorial.   PHOTO BY G.W. CAMPBELL

This obscure botanical garden tops my list of "the most amazing discoveries in Muskoka." Getting to the Dyer Memorial is an adventure in itself. The road winds up hills and around corners, finally dropping like a rollercoaster into the river valley. A stone schoolhouse marks the turnoff into the park. From here a sandy track follows the tortuous curves of the Big East River.

To reach the summit of this Shangri-La, you must then climb a long series of steps flanked by sentinel pines. At the top, an stone monument rises into the sky. Clifton Dyer built the monument as a memorial to his wife Betsy, inscribing it with the words: "An affectionate, loyal and understanding wife is life's greatest gift."

In 1916, the Dyers spent their honeymoon in Algonquin Park. They returned to canoe on Big East River for their 20th anniversary and camped right here. In 1940 the Dyers built a cottage on the bank of the river. The ashes of both Mrs. and Mr. Dyer are in two copper urns at the top of the column. The pillar stands in the centre of a ten-acre park with rolling lawns, a pond and botanical gardens.

Madill United Church.
PHOTO BY G.W. CAMPBELL

8   MADILL CHURCH

(Go south on Highway 11 to the Madill Church Road)

There are not many square-timbered churches left in Ontario. Madill Church is one of them. John Madill donated the land for the church in 1873. Each pioneer in the district contributed two rounds of logs for the building and helped erect the church.

Over the years the local people have kept the church from falling into ruin. In 1935 Mrs. Edward Armstrong (Madill's daughter) redecorated the building at her own expense. In 1968 Wilson Cairns and Les Helstern rebuilt the dry-stone foundation.

The church is a designated historic site. Each July a memorial service is held to honour the early pioneers in the district.

CHAPTER 8

Author's Favourites

— Most Amazing Discovery
  Dyer Memorial

— The Most Scenic Routes —
  Circle Tour of Lake Rosseau
  Side Trip to Dyer Memorial
  South Portage Road (Lake of Bays, A)
  Highway 35 (Lake of Bays, B)
  Muskoka Road 10 (Port Sydney to Huntsville)

— Most Enjoyable Attractions —
  R.M.S. *Segwun*, Gravenhurst
  Muskoka Pioneer Village, Huntsville

— Most Spectacular Lookout (but the scariest climb!) —
  Dorset Lookout Tower

— Most Nostalgic Sight —
  Bigwin Inn

— Favourite Restored Buildings —
  Bethune House, Gravenhurst
  Woodchester Villa, Bracebridge

— Most Neglected Historic Sites —
  Portage Railway/North and South Portage
  Muskoka Wharf

Muskoka Pioneer Village. PHOTO BY G.W. CAMPBELL

South Falls. PHOTO BY SUSAN PRYKE

— Most Interesting Lake —
   Lake of Bays

— Most Dramatic Waterfall —
   South Falls
   High Falls

— Wildest Rapids —
   Oxtongue River Rapids

— Most Impressive Rock Cut —
   Huckleberry Rock Cut, Highway 118

— Best View From A Church —
   St. John the Baptist Church, Morinus

— Most Impressive Pioneer Church —
   All Saints', Huntsville

The steamers Nipissing II and Kenozha docked at Beaumaris.
MUSKOKA LAKES MUSEUM

Bibliography

PRIMARY SOURCES
— Atlas —
Hamilton, W.E., ed. *Guide Book and Atlas of Muskoka and Parry Sound Districts.* Toronto, 1879.

— Government Reports —
Ontario Department of Public Works. *Annual Report, 1914-1918.*

— Lectures —
History of Muskoka District as presented by guest speakers on behalf of Georgian College in Bracebridge, Gravenhurst and Huntsville, October and November 1974, Transcriptions revised and edited by the Algonquin Regional Library System, Parry Sound, 1975.

History of Muskoka District as presented by guest speakers on behalf of Georgian College in Bracebridge, Gravenhurst, Huntsville and Port Carling, September to November 1975. Transcription revised and edited by the Algonquin Regional Library System, Parry Sound, 1976.

— Manuscripts (unpublished) —

Baysville Women's Institute Tweedsmuir History
Laycock, Jack. *Once a Steamboater, Always.*

— Newspapers —
Bracebridge *Herald-Gazette*
Gravenhurst News
Muskoka Advance
Muskoka Sun
Muskokan

— Periodicals and Brochures —
Ontario Motor League Road Books, 1924, 1927, 1934.

SECONDARY SOURCES

Boyer, Robert J. *A Good Town Grew Here.* Bracebridge, 1975,

Boyer, Robert J. Early Exploration and Surveying of Muskoka District. Bracebridge,1979.

Boyer, Robert J. *Woodchester Villa.* Bracebridge, 1982.

Coombe, Geraldine. *Muskoka Past and Present.* Toronto: McGraw-Hill Ryerson, 1976.

Cope, Leila. *A History of the Village of Port Carling.* Bracebridge, 1956.

Denniss, Gary. *A Brief History of the Schools in Muskoka.* Bracebridge, 1972.

Findlay, Mary Lynn. *Lures and Legends of Lake of Bays.* Bracebridge, 1973.

Gravenhurst Historical Committee, Porter, Cecil et al. *The Light of Other Days.* Gravenhurst, 1967.

Haystack Bay Women's Institute Tweedsmuir History. *By Wagon and Water.* Dwight, 1980.

Hutcheson, George F. *Heads and Tales.* Bracebridge, 1972.

Johnson, George H. *Port Sydney Past.* Erin: The Boston Mills Press, 1980.

MacKay, Niall. *By Steam Boat and Steam Train.* Erin: The Boston Mills Press, 1982.

McEachern, Ruth et al. *Dorset.* Bracebridge, 1976.

Murray, Florence B. *Muskoka and Haliburton 1615-1875.* Toronto: University of Toronto Press, 1963.

Research Committee of the Muskoka Pioneer Village, Hunt, Maureen et al. *Pictures From The Past, Huntsville.* Erin: The Boston Mills Press, 1986.

Scovell, Beatrice. *The Muskoka Story* (self-published).

Stott, Derek. *Kawandag.* Rosseau, 1981.

Sutton, F.W. *Early History of Bala.* Bracebridge, 1970.

Tatley, Richard. *The Steamboat Era in the Muskokas, Vol. I & 2.* Erin: The Boston Mills Press,1984.

Index